SIDE CHANNELS
A Collection of Nature Writing and Memoir

To Reggie,

Best wishes,

Thomas V. Lerczak
April 20, 2012

SIDE CHANNELS

A Collection of Nature Writing and Memoir

By Thomas V. Lerczak

Illustrations by Patti Malmborg Reilly

MILL CITY PRESS

Copyright © 2011 by Thomas V. Lerczak

Mill City Press, Inc.
212 3rd Avenue North, Suite 290
Minneapolis, MN 55401
612.455.2294
www.millcitypublishing.com

All rights reserved. No part of this publication may be reproduced, stored in a retrieval system, or transmitted, in any form or by any means, electronic, mechanical, photocopying, recording, or otherwise, without the prior written permission of the author.

ISBN-13: 978-1-936780-37-2
LCCN: 2011927248

Book design by Elsa Engvall

Printed in the United States of America

For Julie

Contents

Foreword ... viii

Introduction ... x

Part One—River Life

1. An Affinity for Rivers ... 1
2. A Sense of Place ... 5
3. Slow and Steady: *A Life of Encounters with Illinois' Great Blue Heron* ... 7
4. Starved Rock and the Illinois River's Locks and Dams ... 13
5. An Illinois River Canoeing Journal: *Nature's Ways on Illinois' Busy Waterway* ... 17
6. Illinois' Continental Divide: *Mud Lake and the Chicago Portage* ... 23
7. Timeless Scenes Along the Illinois River ... 25
8. Bald Eagles on a Morning Commute ... 31
9. The Eagle Quest ... 33
10. Wings Over the River: *A Portrait of Illinois' Swallows* ... 37
11. First Glimpse of the Upper Mississippi River Valley ... 45
12. A Lesson in Nature's Dynamics: Barton-Sommer's Woodland ... 49
13. Dead Trees, Disturbance, and Illinois' Red-headed Woodpeckers ... 57
14. From the Misery Index to Havana ... 67
15. The Shorebirds Among Us ... 71
16. When Hawks Fly ... 77
17. Carrying on an Electro-shocking Legacy ... 85
18. Nature Along the Margins at Cooper Park Wetlands ... 91
19. As the Rivers Rise Again ... 99
20. The Gizzard Shad in Nature's Economy ... 103

21. In Praise of Sitting and Staring ... 110

Part Two—Travel

22. Pursuing the Blue Goose Across Illinois ... 115
23. Eulogy for an Oak ... 127
24. Drawn to Antiquity ... 135
25. A Western Birding Excursion: Of Wind, Rain, Rocks, and Renewal ... 139
26. Ties ... 151
27. From a Great Lakes Journal: Of Sand, Glaciers, and Birds ... 155
28. Encounters with the Niagara River ... 165
29. Taking in the American Bottom ... 169
30. Isle Royale: A Wilderness Island in Lake Superior ... 173

Epilogue: *Thoughts on Twenty-five Years as a Naturalist* ... 181

Acknowledgments ... 185

Foreword

By Debbie S. Newman

When I sat down to begin reading *Side Channels*, I decided to put on some Native American flute music. Rock n' roll music would have been too distracting from the task at hand. But as the words of the essays began to unfold in front of me, what I had chosen for some "background" music suddenly seemed like it was made for the book. Or was the book made for the music? Whichever, it was like milk and cookies, a perfect match of flavors and textures. From the beginning, Tom Lerczak managed to transport me with him on an odyssey of sorts, rich in the infinite mélange of a natural world many people hardly know. Like much Native American music, adventures in this book evoke a strong sense of place that is transcendent of time and space. Tom illustrates that there are many parts to any story, showing us a river or landscape today, and then taking us to that same place 40 years ago, or 10,000 years ago; viewing that river from underwater as would a fish, and then from above through the eyes of an eagle. After reading these stories, you will be certain in the back of your mind that you've actually visited these places.

I was delighted when Tom asked me to write a foreword for his book. I've long been familiar with his writing. He first began refining his naturalist writing skills when I was editing *Illinois Audubon* magazine for the Illinois Audubon Society. Tom sent me articles with a deep sense of the details found in nature—described from an astute eye. As Tom polished his workmanship, these details showed that he is a true student of the wild.

Not that this was a surprise to me.

I first met Tom through my husband, Barry Newman, whom Tom worked with at the Illinois Natural History Survey. We quickly became good friends, spending time together on shared passions such as bird watching. It was here that I saw Tom's penchant for observing the details of nature. Me being sometimes a rather impatient person, I was always reminded by accompanying Tom that patience and quiet observation—nearly a lost art in our world today—are the true keys to experiencing the finer details of nature, and are essential to painting the word-pictures found in this book of essays.

Tom and I were fortunate enough to commence working for the Illinois Nature Preserves Commission simultaneously in the 1990s. Working for the Commission is a pleasure, because it is an adventure. Tom shares in this book what we both know as Commission staff: living a life of loving nature leads to one adventure after another, whether in the company of an old oak friend or a cadre of winged companions, or atop an ancient, grass-covered bluff. I invite you to join these adventures through Tom's words. Read, and enjoy!

Debbie S. Newman
December, 2009

Bend in the River

Introduction

Ideas about our relationship with nature...[are] confused by wish, want-to-be, and imaginary worlds that have never existed.
–from Strange Encounters, by Daniel B. Botkin

Given enough ingenuity, a scientist can make practically any scheme sound plausible.
–from The Life of an Oak, An Intimate Portrait, by Glenn Keator

In 1993, I began occasionally writing what became popular articles on nature-related topics. Although birds were the focus for many of the articles, most also touched on various aspects of the science of ecology; topics included evolution, plant succession, habitat partitioning, food webs, the role of fire and disturbance in oak-dominated habitats, and river ecology. This book contains fourteen of those previously published articles, which have been updated and revised only slightly from their original texts.

Because I have long had an interest in rivers and wild places, the Illinois River, which flows through a mostly rural part of Illinois, is a common backdrop for many of the articles; and the idea of wilderness, or some aspect of a quality called "wildness," is touched upon more than a few times, especially in the context of finding such a quality in a highly domesticated state such as Illinois. So while each article was written independently of the others, there is a common thread running through all of them.

When I first thought of collecting these articles together into a book, I still felt that something more was necessary to tie everything together and perhaps better allow the reader to approach the book as a whole. Toward this end, I began writing a series of short memoir pieces, twelve in all, that examine the roots of my fascination with rivers and wild areas. They illustrate how my perspectives on nature and human society have changed over the years, from the typical naivety of youth to what I hope is a mature, common sense outlook, with a minimum of illusions, based on hard-won knowledge and objectivity. Perhaps others with a similar interest in nature, who may be frustrated by their circumstances of living in areas where publicly accessible natural lands may be few and far between or diminishing, may benefit by reading about how one man was able to bring together seemingly disparate, incompatible aspects of his life to find a balance—for want of a better word—with nature as the center, even where influences of modernity were never far away.

The chapters in this book are arranged into two major sections. The experiences written about in *Part One—River Life* occurred in Illinois, mostly along or near the Illinois River and its tributaries. *Part Two—Travel* documents journeys I have taken searching for wild areas and birds in Illinois as well as in the western states, the upper Midwest, and the Great Lakes region. Scattered throughout the book are fourteen line drawings by artist Patti Malmborg Reilly of Maine.

Part One

River Life

Mouth of the Spoon River, Illinois

I
An Affinity for Rivers

Having been drawn to rivers for most of my life, I have only recently begun to contemplate the origins of this attraction and whether it may be similar for others. And I have decided that the attraction is there because a river is a natural presence and a process, an entity in fact, on our domesticated landscapes, winding through distance as well as time. The flowing waters of rivers are carried from the far reaches of their headwaters, always interconnecting with other rivers, tributaries, and finally the sea; each is merely one stage in the great cycle of water, connected to the skies above, set into perpetual motion from the sun's limitless radiance. And waters have flowed over the meandering beds of rivers, through one course or another, ever since water has flowed over our earth. Though changed, and in most cases degraded, from our manipulations, rivers still provide us with these natural links to a timeless process.

* * *

My fascination with rivers began in the mid-1960s in Chicago, Illinois. I grew up in a neighborhood that was typical of the older parts of most large cities: rectangular city blocks; small bungalows with small back yards; houses separated by only a few feet, called "gangways;" corner "mom-and-pop" grocery stores; and a field of view not much further than the houses across the narrow street. My compact world was secure, mowed, trimmed, under control, predictable, and all within view or within a short walk. I cannot imagine that I ever thought much about what was beyond this safe environment, and if I did, television took care of that.

During the summer months, we would occasionally attend large picnic affairs organized by my grandparents' Czechoslovakian fellowship club held at the National Grove Forest Preserve in Riverside, a small Chicago suburb. My maternal grandparents came to the United States from Czechoslovakia (now the Czech Republic) in 1920, and these picnics gave them a way to stay in touch with other Czech-Americans and to keep their culture alive. There was Czech food, the Czech language spoken freely, and accordion-led polka bands. The concrete dance floor in the pavilion was sometimes packed with frail elderly women dancing with each other, shuffling across the floor and barely lifting their feet. Their husbands were probably unwilling to dance, or perhaps they had already passed away.

While I would find all of these activities interesting today, at the time my thoughts—such as they must have been—were already elsewhere. Just beyond the shaded picnic tables and mowed field, the forests were quite untamed, waiting for exploration. I, of course, had never seen anything like those wild, tangled forests, and I was quite taken with this strange wilderness scene not very far from my home.

Though my parents came to the picnics to socialize and soak in the culture, during every visit it was not long before my brother and I begged and nagged to be taken for a walk through "the woods," as we called them. The forests were dense and shaded, and seemed not to be under anyone's care or control, growing as chance circumstances dictated—a very appealing temptation for a boy of seven or eight years old. But as unlike my Chicago neighborhood as these forests were, it was really the Des Plaines River, at the furthest part of our walks, that truly captivated my imagination and, as I look back, set my interests on a trajectory that continues.

Before getting near to the river, I recall that it was possible to smell it in the air; not an unpleasant aroma, it was one of mud, humidity, and decaying organic matter from the bottomland forests. (The Des Plaines River was quite polluted at that time, before much attention was given to water quality, but we were scarcely aware of that, and the river did not betray its dark secrets.) I remember standing at the riverside, watching the river's smooth, moving surface, throwing sticks into the river as far as possible to see them float away downstream. I wondered where the river came from—surely from some vast wilderness forest upstream—and where it went, not hearing for even a moment the busy traffic on First Avenue about 100 yards beyond the opposite bank. And I guess I already knew that rivers flowed eventually to the sea.

I could have stayed at the river's bank until after dark. But my parents were always eager to return to the picnic celebrations. So, reluctantly following behind, I immediately and eagerly looked forward to the next weekend's picnic and a return to the river. My lifelong interest in rivers—possibly also my independent ways and wanderlust—began at this very river. And I believe that I am finally beginning to understand why.

Side Channels

2

A Sense of Place

A glance at any map of North America shows that the Midwest is a landscape of rivers, with the Mississippi as its centerpiece. On the Mississippi River's watershed—from the Allegheny River in New York and Pennsylvania to the headwaters of the Missouri River in Montana to the obscure birth of the Mississippi River itself at Lake Itasca, Minnesota—traveling across Middle America, one is never far from flowing waters.

My home lies fairly in the central portion of and in the middle of this well-watered river basin, a few miles east of the Illinois River, one of the Mississippi's many tributaries. The Illinois River valley and adjacent largely-forested bluff lands are quite unlike the gently rolling to flat landscape of central Illinois, dominated as it is by expanses of farmland, largely of corn and soybean. The Illinois River is a force on the landscape through which it travels, though it is a much lesser river (by any measure) than the Mississippi.

The headwaters of the Illinois River arise in the greater Chicago metropolitan area and northwestern Indiana, with the Des Plaines and Kankakee rivers the two main feeder streams. Then 273 miles downstream, the Illinois joins the Mississippi River opposite the town of Grafton, Illinois, about 20 miles upstream from where the Missouri River also joins the Mississippi. In between, the Illinois River valley corridor provides a wonderful sense of place with discernable boundaries, a beginning and an end.

Towboat-barge on the Illinois River

3

Slow and Steady:
A Life of Encounters with Illinois' Great Blue Heron

The sudden appearance of a great blue heron on the scene cannot be ignored. Standing four feet tall on spindly legs, with a long, snake-like neck and head ending in a spear-like bill, a six-foot wingspan, and the serious eyes of an unforgiving predator, the bird commands attention. And so, what else could I, as a seven- or eight-year-old boy, do but look upward when this strange creature flew overhead, following Nippersink Creek in northeastern Illinois? With awe and, as I recall, not a small degree of fear, I watched as the large awkward-looking bird flew onward. In the years between then and now the species has flown in and out of my life many times; and with each appearance it has left impressions and influences. Great blue herons exemplify steadfastness, an ability to endure hardships, and what I interpret as patience. And if I have been able to incorporate such admirable qualities into my life as a result of encounters with this species, then I have perhaps lived a better life.

For many years after that initial sighting, the Nippersink Creek during summer was the only place that I had seen great blue herons, though the widespread and common birds must have often been on the periphery of view, flying high overhead or off to the side, or simply hiding in the shadows. Though herons may readily be found along streams and marshes, they are at the same time rare in or totally absent from highly urbanized areas, and that was where I lived during my younger years and where I spent most of my time. But the whole truth is that my focus was elsewhere, least of all on great blue herons, or more likely nowhere at all.

Herons, though, managed to make occasional appearances nonetheless. One morning, for example, in the late 1970s, as I walked toward my Berwyn alleyway with its telephone poles, overhead wires, garages, and rusty garbage cans, a harsh squawk broke into my day dreams; and for less than a minute, I stood in shock as a gangly, gray-blue creature took flight and then quickly disappeared over the rooftops. Telling the story later to friends and family drew only polite smiles; still, I knew that I had seen such a creature before; and in my mind's eye, I could still see my first encounter with the bird well over ten years before.

A year or so after the alley incident, on the Fox River in northern Illinois, I took my first canoe trip. Here, great blue herons were a common sight, usually standing quietly along the river's banks, trying to remain inconspicuous. But when my canoe floated closer than a heron might consider a comfortable distance, the bird would emit its characteristic squawk, fly downstream a few hundred yards, and then repeat the same behavior as the flowing waters carried my canoe downstream and inevitably toward the waiting heron. Sometimes a heron would eventually backtrack to its original location, which, I surmised, had been a feeding territory. During these canoe trips, I admired the herons' persistence after being repeatedly disturbed along the popular canoeing river; they seemed determined to continue using the river as their species had always done since before history. I thought of them, in fact, as links to the past, to a simpler time when the pace of a canoe was also the pace at which, I imagined, most folks lived their lives.

Those river day trips and heron encounters drew me closer to nature at a critical time during my early twenties, when I was searching for my place in the world. These days, with the Illinois River valley and its array of aquatic habitats close to home, a great blue heron sighting can be a daily occurrence throughout the year, should I choose to make even the slightest effort by simply scanning along the river banks on any given day. Outside of the winter months, the other of Illinois' heron and egret species may also be sighted along the river valley. The great egret's pure white plumage stands out against the background wherever they happen to be, and sometimes they may be found in great numbers, along with great blue herons, at preferred roost trees or shallow-water feeding areas. Other species, such as the green heron and black-crowned night heron, may take a bit more searching. Little blue herons, snowy egrets, and cattle egrets become more obvious mostly just after the breeding season, when individuals disperse along the Illinois River valley in search of forage before their final southward migrations out of Illinois. Species such as the American bittern, least bittern, and yellow-crowned night heron, on the other hand, can be so elusive that years may pass between sightings. Only the great blue heron, with its slow and steady plodding flight, is reliable, and that is not a bad trait. The bird's flight, especially against the wind, is a good reminder to me that sometimes progress is gradual, and by working hard and consistently, one's goals in life may ultimately not be denied.

One August day I sat in the shade of a tree with the sun behind, just on the edge of an old Spoon River oxbow, a former river channel that had been cut off from the main river long ago. Flood waters were still draining toward the river in places; but fish were being trapped in the isolated, remnant pools of flood waters. Great blue herons and great egrets, unaware of my presence, stood in the shallow waters of the oxbow, motionless or walking so slowly that their movements were barely perceptible. What great patience these birds had, as their legs and feet moved with the water, not even causing the slightest ripple, hoping as they were to fool any nearby fish into feelings of safety. Time seemed suspended, my attention challenged by having to drag out each additional moment; and then, about when my impatience no longer allowed me to watch, with laser-guided precision, the heron nearest to me (about 50 feet away) swiftly speared a small fish (about six inches in length) on its bill, quickly re-positioned the fish, and then swallowed it whole, all within a few seconds. And a moment later, the same heron caught another fish nearly the same size as the first, and then another, and still another. Before me was a scene that illustrated the old adage that patience has its rewards. But that was not all, because patience without the ability to strike with unerring accuracy and unexpected speed would have resulted only in more waiting; and swiftly striking willy-nilly would have simply been a waste of energy; it was the combination of both that, in the end, won the day.

When the Illinois River leaves its banks in a major flood—usually at least once a year, especially during spring—many areas of the river valley that are not protected by levees become inaccessible except by watercraft. During such times, wild creatures, of course, must adapt to what the environment delivers or leave in search of better habitats; some, such as the great blue heron, adapt very well. When shallow-water habitats are few and far between, herons may use tree limbs protruding from the water as foraging perches. They may even somewhat awkwardly dive, or rather, land hard into the water to catch prey, and then swim toward shore, or even ungracefully rise from the water's surface in a confusion of wings, legs, outstretched neck, and splashing water. Of course, great blue herons excel at the slow and steady stealth-hunting along the margins of a clear-water marsh or river, where they are able to capitalize on their unique characteristics in favorable circumstances. But the great blue heron's ability to adapt to a variety of situations is, without a doubt, one of the reasons why they have remained successful compared to similar, less adaptable, and declining species, such as the American bittern.

One cold, mid-winter day, I walked along the Spoon River toward its confluence with the Illinois River. The weather had been below freezing for quite some time, and the Spoon River's surface was frozen. Wildlife was scarce, and I kept up a brisk pace to help generate warmth just as the cold winds stole it away. As I rounded the final curve of the Spoon River, I looked down the river's steep 10-foot-high banks just as a group of 15 or 20 great blue herons standing below the river banks flew from their safe haven from the biting north winds. As they flew from my presence, I thought about them enduring day after cold day during a long winter and somehow finding enough food to make it worthwhile to stay in the area, rather than moving further south with the other heron and egret species. Being tough and enduring the bad times: something every living thing must deal with sooner or later.

When winter ends, the great blue herons are almost immediately thrust into the challenges of the breeding season, when they choose new mates each year and build large stick nests in the canopies of floodplain forests. During this period, they gather into colonies of a few to several hundred nests, but they also nest as single pairs. Large colonies provide better protection from predation than isolated nests. But large colonies are notorious for their strange cacophony of sounds, as if the birds are being strangled to death; continual tumult from the constant incoming and outgoing parent birds; putrid stench of rotting fish, heron excrement, and decaying bodies of fallen nestlings; and the unimaginably great numbers of insects, especially the biting buffalo gnats, that are drawn to such attractions. But somehow the birds endure the rookery experience, and each spring they are ready for more. Of course, it is instinct that causes them to return to their breeding behaviors, not a nagging personal responsibility to sacrifice in the name of perpetuating the species; yet I cannot help but appreciate their ability to suffer hardship—whether it is a choice or not.

* * *

As the six lanes of expressway traffic moved quickly along Interstate 55 near Chicago, wisps of vehicles continually changed lanes in front and in back of me, passing me, and slowing down. My conscious attention was, by necessity, riveted to keeping up with the flow. But having just left my father's funeral, my thoughts were elsewhere, filled as they were with a kaleidoscope of images and words: my father smiling and laughing, cooking Sunday dinners, taking my brother and me on hikes in the Cook County Forest Preserves, and his ultimate good-bye two weeks earlier that I hoped would not be final. And then I saw the heron, flying over the traffic and dense urban sprawl of warehouses, parking lots, shopping centers, homes, and more roads. I had a dim image in my mind of that first great blue heron over the Nippersink Creek so many years before, a time when my parents were much younger than I myself was on that funereal day. And I said to my wife, "Look! Look at that heron flying." The bird seemed oblivious to all that occurred beneath its flight path; methodically and calmly flying along, the heron went about its business, simply going on with its life. And I knew, just as simply, that I had to do the same.

4

Starved Rock and the Illinois River's Locks and Dams

The Illinois River came into view as I approached the base of Starved Rock, just before beginning a daunting climb with my father and brother to the top of the rock, 125 feet above the river. It was the first time I had visited Starved Rock State Park, sometime in the middle 1960s, and the first time I had seen the Illinois River. A short distance upstream of the rock, the crashing, turbulent waters of the river passed through the partially open gates of the Starved Rock Dam. Behind the dam, the water spread out into a large lake nearly one mile wide and seemed, to all appearances, stagnant. Was this a river, as I had been informed? I was quite familiar with the sluggish Des Plaines River coursing through the forest preserves near my Chicago home, and that river flowed freely. So the body of water before me only vaguely seemed like a river; not even the dam seemed consistent with the image in my mind of what a dam should be: a large concrete wall completely holding back a large body of water, with nary a drop of water making it through the dam. What purpose, I thought at the time, could there be for a dam that allowed a torrent of water to pass through?

Of course, the answer, as I discovered years later, is that the Illinois River is a regulated, highly managed river, not a natural free-flowing river; water flows and levels are carefully manipulated by the U.S. Army Corps of Engineers to maintain a commercial navigation channel to a minimum depth of 9 feet. The Starved Rock Dam, in fact, is one of five similar navigation dams built in the 1930s along the Illinois River that work together—opening and closing gates, holding back water or letting it through—to allow barges and other watercraft to ply the river's waters throughout the year, droughts notwithstanding. Each navigation dam has an accompanying lock chamber that allows river traffic to bypass the dams. Without the navigation dams, the river would frequently become too shallow for large crafts to navigate, and the rapids at Starved Rock and Marseilles, now submerged beneath backed-up water behind the dams—referred to as *navigation pools*—would remain insurmountable barriers.

But such engineering technicalities aside, from atop Starved Rock, one cannot help but be pensive, literally standing upon history, with thoughts pulled back hundreds of years. Names such as La Salle, Hennepin, Tonti, Marquette, and Illiniwek float in the air and are written upon park landmarks and trail heads. Yet all around the park, the modern works of man cannot be ignored, and one may wonder what the river and its valley might be like hundreds of years into the future, how primitive today's view from the rock would be to a hyper-technological society with everyday contrivances unimaginable during our era, much as cell phones and wireless Internet on laptop computers would have been unimaginable to the French explorers of the seventeenth century.

Today Starved Rock seems less impressive and less massive to me than it did over four decades ago. And though the park may be slightly more developed around the lodge and day-use parking areas, it otherwise remains much as I first experienced. In the intervening years, I have traveled the length of the river valley many times; canoed the river's waters; explored its backwaters, bluffs, and floodplain forests; studied its ecology; and lamented its degradation as an unfortunate consequence of modern prosperity and progress. Yet, despite my travels elsewhere, before too long, I always return to Starved Rock, though sometimes several years may pass between visits. The rock certainly is the main attraction, but perhaps it is also the dam that draws my attention, as it did many years ago. Today I see the dam as it is juxtaposed against the backdrop of natural beauty and history preserved at the park, a poignant reminder of our power to manipulate and manage the environment, while also recognizing limits and consequences. Few places—certainly not the river's other locks and dams—generate such inspiration, and maybe that is why I continue to return often and remember.

Side Channels

5

An Illinois River Canoeing Journal:
Nature's Ways on Illinois' Busy Waterway

Without a doubt, I am drawn toward rivers in part because of their connections to faraway places. Rarely do I look upon the Illinois River, for example, without imagining its headwaters in Chicago and its waters flowing to the Mississippi River and eventually the Gulf of Mexico. And the river valley is a hotspot for bird life, with certain species conjuring up images of fantastically distant locations, from South America to the Arctic tundra. This sense of time and distance seems even more the case in a quiet canoe, lazily floating along with the current. The connection to the greater landscape is quite obvious.

Yet the Illinois River is not without its challenges. Huge towboats that push numerous barges (towboat-barges) ply its waters throughout the year transporting vast loads of commodities such as grain and coal, which may have ultimate destinations throughout the world. In the summer months, its main channel is an adult playground for the full spectrum of motorboats, from swift personal watercraft to wave-producing cruisers to partying pontoon boats. A daydreaming canoeist could easily be swallowed up in a noisy whirlpool of activity.

Seven miles downstream from Havana, however, one may find respite. Here is six-mile-long, privately owned Grand Island. Such large islands are rare along the Illinois River; most are much shorter and quite narrow. Though the island is not open for public access, along Grand Island's eastern flank is an Illinois River side channel called Bath Chute. Access is from the main river on the upstream and downstream ends of the island and from a public boat ramp in the small river town of Bath. In Bath Chute, it is possible to return to nature's pace, where seeing a soaring red-tailed hawk may be the highest priority rather than being swamped in the main river by a three-foot swell, or precariously riding out boat-generated waves in deeper water, like an aquatic rodeo.

The word "chute" implies fast-moving water down a steep, narrow incline. But the current in Bath Chute is usually sluggish. At Bath's boat ramp one late September morning, I reviewed the options. One option would be to float four miles downstream to the lower end of Grand Island, and then paddle back against the weak current. Another option would be to circumnavigate the island, at least a 12-mile trip, six of which would be along the main Illinois River. From experience, I knew that this could be a tough trip if the wind picked up and if the river were busy. With a goal of being off the river well before noon, I decided to follow Bath Chute upstream, against the current, two miles to the Illinois River at the head of Grand Island. The return trip would be an easy float.

After paddling a short distance upstream from the boat ramp, where the channel gently curves to the northwest, the riverside residences of Bath were soon left behind. The natural settings on both sides of the channel shifted my mind away from the modern world, to an earlier time when the rest of the river looked similar to what I was then seeing. The gently meandering channel almost had a hypnotic effect, where I would occasionally switch back and forth to either side of the channel to stay on the inside of the curves, for slower water or to dodge wind gusts.

Here the floodplain forests are extensive and thick, with tall cottonwood, green ash, and silver maple trees that hang over the channel margins and provide habitat for a diverse bird community. I occasionally saw pileated and red-headed woodpeckers flying over the channel, and heard them calling several times throughout the day. At one point, a barred owl sounded off one call and then went silent. Carolina wrens sang throughout the day, as they tend to do at all times of the year, sometimes making fall days seem like spring. And tree swallows, perhaps bound for the Mexican coast, stocked up on energy (i.e., insects) for the long flights ahead.

Log jams along the banks and sunken trees in the middle of the meandering channel add to the natural aspect of Bath Chute. On several occasions a single branch extending above the waterline from a sunken tree, referred to as a "sawyer," bobbed up and down because of the current flow. The sunken trees or snags provide good structure for fish habitat, especially in a muddy stream such as the Illinois, and turtles use the logs to bask in the sun. Our rivers originally had great quantities of such woody debris before the rivers were cleared for navigation. Bath Chute makes it easy to imagine what the Illinois River used to look like before the steamboat era.

Although there are times when Bath Chute can be a bit busy with anglers, this trip was typical of my usual experience of quiet days, especially in the fall and spring. The occasional johnboat may quickly pass, with the driver typically slowing down for canoeists, but there are long stretches of time with only the sounds of the wind, birds, and the canoe paddle slicing through the water. During one such time, I found a place to wedge the canoe between a few branches of a sunken tree, and sat back to read a book and scan the skies.

On late September days, it is not uncommon to see hundreds of American white pelicans in migration, spiraling upward on air thermals to great heights, far beyond sight of the unaided eye. While my canoe was secured against the snag, I glanced at several such "pelican thermals," and noticed about ten broad-winged hawks rising on another nearby thermal. If conditions are right, great numbers of these hawks may take to the skies at once, creating quite an impressive sight. These birds overwinter as far as southern Peru or Brazil. A spotted sandpiper, walking and foraging on a log, completed the feeling of being connected to both hemispheres; they breed as far north as the high Arctic and winter as far south as Argentina.

After sitting for a while, I carefully lifted myself from the bottom of the canoe and continued paddling toward the Illinois River. My movements caused a belted kingfisher to call and take flight, and several great blue herons and great egrets spooked as I passed. Some of the herons would remain all winter, but the egrets would move to the Gulf Coast and beyond.

A towboat-barge was passing upstream as I neared the head of Grand Island at river mile 113.3 (i.e., that many miles from the Mississippi River). In its wake, I ventured across the open river, which seemed quite large compared with the chute. An osprey, somewhat resembling a gull in flight just as the field guides state, leisurely flew southward, closely following the river. And there were numerous blue-winged teal, mallards, and wood ducks flying in all directions. But while the bird life was exciting, my attention and exertion were focused on the canoe as the wind began picking up speed and gusting, creating small whitecaps, and turning the canoe in the wrong direction if my thoughts strayed for even a second.

Eventually reaching the river's opposite bank, I beached the canoe and hiked to the top of a high levee that parallels the river all the way to Havana. Parts of the levee are lined with piles of boulders (rip-rap) as protection from wave action during floods. Beyond the levee, rich farmlands stretched for miles. The river valley bluffs were clearly visible three miles to the west, and the Spoon River bluffs with Dickson Mounds Museum were visible ten miles northward. Though my thoughts were focused on nature and how the river used to be, seeing the museum and recalling its fine archaeological exhibits reminded me that human societies had occupied this river valley for thousands of years. Once again, the river is the common thread, weaving time and distance with the day's experiences.

Ancient civilizations, Peruvian forests, Arctic tundra. How my mind's eye traveled without much prompting. But I promised myself to be home by noon, to attend to the necessities of this life. And so I crossed the river back to Bath Chute, fighting the wind as before, for a light float back to the boat ramp. On the way, I kept expecting to be jerked to attention by a jumping Asian silver carp, a large, abundant, exotic species that tends to jump into canoes and even fast-moving speedboats. But either they were not around or they were not motivated to jump. Who knows what motivates a fish to jump out of the water. Temperature changes? Rising water? Time of year? Engine vibrations? All of the above? I noticed a few dead silver carp on the river banks; so at least scavenging bald eagles, turkey vultures, crows, and gulls seem to have an additional food resource.

When the Boat Tavern—a converted barge high on stilts near the boat ramp—came into view, my canoe trip was nearly over. I knew the folks inside were watching me return and would ask questions when I ordered a cool beverage to drink while loading up my gear. The Grand Island circumnavigation still beckons, but it must wait for a day when I have more energy and time, perhaps some cold fall day when the river is calm, birds are on the move, and my urge to be on the river just simply will not let me make it to the office.

Side Channels

6

Illinois' Continental Divide:
Mud Lake and the Chicago Portage

Long before Chicago was settled by Americans of European descent and the landscape became highly altered, the Mississippi River and Great Lakes basins were separated by a shallow marshy area called Mud Lake. This prairie marsh fed into the Chicago River, which, at that time, flowed into Lake Michigan. (The Great Lakes' waters empty into the North Atlantic Ocean via the St. Lawrence River.) The nearby Des Plaines River flows toward the Illinois River, the Mississippi River, and ultimately the Gulf of Mexico. The Chicago Portage, a traveler's trail across the Mud Lake marsh, was located at the point where the Des Plaines and Chicago rivers were at their closest approach. The strategic importance of this site was never obscure to anyone, least of all the Native Americans.

Never far from the Illinois River during most of the last two decades, it seems somehow appropriate that I spent most of my childhood days literally on land long ago reclaimed from Mud Lake at the headwaters of the Illinois River. I recall myself as a boy nosing around railroad yards and abandoned land beyond the safe boundaries of Chicago's Lawndale Park, excited by small pools of clear water with cattails and crayfish. These pools must have been the most difficult areas to fully drain, and today I am convinced that they were remnants of Mud Lake itself.

My parents forbade me to wander beyond the "back of the park," as we used to say. There were dangers, no doubt, as the burned out hobo campfires, discarded whiskey bottles, and occasional dead dog attested. And most of the time, I followed their rules.

These days, passing over the Stevenson Expressway (Interstate 55) near Chicago and seeing the sewage treatment plant, ship canal, factories, roads, businesses, and homes, it is nearly impossible to imagine Mud Lake and its environs 300 or more years ago. The location of the Chicago Portage is now marked as a historic landmark, located west of busy Harlem Avenue, where one can walk through the forest preserve on well-worn trails to the Des Plaines River. Engineers had long ago reversed the direction of the Chicago River, and it now flows into the Chicago Sanitary and Ship Canal; then, southwest of the Chicago area, into the Des Plaines River. Yet a dedicated adventurer may still be able to find those small pools of clear water with cattails beyond the Lawndale Park boundaries, where unknown dangers are likely to still lurk. The rest lives only in the history books.

7
Timeless Scenes Along the Illinois River

With much of the Midwest being devoted to agriculture, an expansive highway infrastructure, and the expanding sprawl of urban areas, it is easy to think of every aspect of the landscape as being tamed and dominated by human desires and manipulations. But every once in a while, large flood events, such as the Great Flood of 1993 on the Mississippi River system, have shown us otherwise, at least for areas on the floodplain; in fact, between the big river bluffs, an ancient play of nature continues (in its fundamentals), most likely unchanged for millennia. The play involves bald eagles, which are top predators in the system, and their prey, mostly fish and to a lesser extent ducks. In Illinois, the large number of bald eagles that overwinter along the Illinois River each year from about late October to March provides an opportunity for observers to learn much about animal behavior, or at least to renew an appreciation of wild nature, unconstrained by human influences.

At Swan Lake, a backwater at the Two Rivers National Wildlife Refuge near the Illinois River's confluence with the Mississippi, for example, I once observed several eagles standing on the ice near a large flock of snow geese. It seemed that the eagles were closely scanning the geese. During most interactions between bald eagles and waterfowl, the eagles appear to be testing the flocks for weak or injured individuals. Every now and then an eagle would fly over the geese causing the entire flock of several hundred to simultaneously take flight. The geese flew as a large ill-defined mass, circled the area, and then landed close to their original place, near the watching eagles. One other winter at Goose Lake, along the Illinois River north of Peoria, I saw a similar sequence of events between an immature eagle and a densely packed flock of several hundred mallards. Like the snow geese, the ducks were engaging in anti-predator behavior. One of the functions of flocking, it seems, is to present a confusion of moving bodies, making it difficult to pick out a single individual. Schooling fish use the same tactic. This interpretation seems to make sense, and was supported by another observation I made at Chautauqua National Wildlife Refuge, about 40 miles southwest of Peoria.

On the surface of Chautauqua Refuge's frozen lake, there was a large group of bald eagles, American crows, ring-billed gulls, and ducks. Most of the ducks were mallards that were standing on the ice in a close-knit flock or floating in a dense pack within a patch of open water. Several eagles stood around the periphery of the ducks a short distance away. My spotting scope was trained on an adult eagle that was soaring so high that it was almost beyond sight. Suddenly, the eagle went into a steep dive. I kept the spotting scope trained on the bird, and so was not looking ahead as to what might have been the cause for the dive. Then, in a rather ungainly fashion, the eagle attempted to come straight down onto a pair of mallards that were separated from the main flock by several hundred meters. The mallards scattered by running in two different directions; and shortly thereafter, the female made a fatal mistake: she took flight. The eagle soon caught up to the female mallard and attempted a mid-air catch, forcing the duck straight down to the ice. There was a short scurry between the two birds before the eagle, with little effort, completed the kill. Then immediately, an immature eagle was on the scene. But the adult eagle jumped away with the duck in its talons and proceeded to feed, ripping at the duck with its hooked beak and sending feathers flying in all directions. Meanwhile, the drake continued to stand alone in an exposed position on the open ice. Just as I retrained my scope on the drake, a different adult eagle came at it from the side with a terrific force, killing it instantly. Another adult eagle then arrived on the scene and was able to steal the duck carcass. Then an immature eagle arrived and attempted to steal the carcass, which caused the adult to fly away with the duck in its talons.

During the winter, bald eagles, it seems, are probably as likely to steal food from other birds as they are to catch their own, even though food may be very abundant. Another example of food stealing occurred at this same site with an American crow that was struggling to swallow a fish, and was repeatedly pursued by an eagle standing nearby. The crow, carrying its fish, hopped a few feet away from the eagle, but the eagle always followed. Eventually the crow flew away, with the fish in its beak. Much of the time, however, especially when feeding on gizzard shad, little stealing or squabbling for food occurs among the eagles, and they more or less hunt in a solitary manner, foraging on whatever is available.

On another occasion, though, at Chautauqua Refuge, during a subfreezing winter day, when a patch of water was kept open by flowing through a broken levee, food must have been readily available; most of the birds were seen feeding on small gizzard shad. An adult eagle flew over a group of ducks, mostly common mergansers, many of which were feeding on the abundant shad. The mergansers curiously appeared unconcerned at having such a formidable predator within easy reach, while the eagle effortlessly picked a medium-sized (15-25 centimeters) shad from the water, ignoring the ducks. The eagle flew to the nearby ice to feed. In a few seconds, an immature eagle was after the adult. An aerial chase occurred for several minutes until the immature eagle gave up, and the adult flew out of sight, still holding its fish. Nearby, a large dead fish (probably a bigmouth buffalo or common carp) was on the ice near the open water. Several eagles stood nearby. After a short time, an adult claimed the fish; while facing the other eagles, the adult threw its head back and called. No sooner had it begun to feed when, from a distant location, an immature eagle aggressively flew at the adult, forcing it from the fish. The fish changed possession among several immature eagles for the next hour or so; at one point, two of them were simultaneously driven away from the fish by a third eagle. Far from this activity, other eagles stood on the ice with no apparent relation to or interest in ducks or open water. One would think they would be drawn to where the action was taking place, near the ducks or open water where dead shad might be easily seen floating on the surface. Perhaps they were closely watching the other birds, waiting for a chance to obtain another bird's catch.

These interpretations of eagle and duck behavior invite many questions. Were the watching eagles really assessing the ducks for weaknesses, or is some other interpretation more plausible? Why did the snow geese and mallards take flight when an eagle passed low overhead, but the mergansers did not? The answer may possibly be that because mergansers are diving ducks, they can quickly go far below the water should an eagle show signs of attempting an attack; mallards are dabbling ducks and more buoyant, less able to seek the underwater as a refuge. Perhaps the eagles and ducks both knew this.

In our society, stealing is considered wrong and bad. Should eagle behavior be judged by our standards or not judged at all? In our evaluation, we must avoid rank anthropomorphism. It is known that successful survival through the winter is directly related to successful breeding the following season. And passing favorable traits (for example, the bald eagle's propensity to steal food) onto successive generations is, after all, the basis for the most powerful and all-pervasive force in nature: natural selection. Individuals lacking the favorable traits can be expected to produce less offspring. With this perspective, stealing food is merely a survival tactic, reflecting an opportunistic foraging strategy that has been shaped by natural selection.

Yet unequivocal answers to questions concerning animal behavior may ultimately prove elusive. All we have are interpretations of their behavior. Perhaps, though, it is enough to simply ask the questions, to acknowledge that despite the apparent tameness of our Midwestern landscape, the character of wildness endures here and there, wherever the habitat remains. And for the habitat to remain is, of course, an important point.

Side Channels

Eagle Bluff at Chautauqua National Wildlife Refuge, Illinois

8

Bald Eagles on a Morning Commute

On mornings in late December, the sun rises late and the alarm clock sounds while it is still dark outside. It's tough to drag my complaining bones out of a warm bed to make my way downstairs to start water boiling for coffee. Though I've always been attracted to lands far north of Illinois, on cold winter mornings before sunrise, the last place I would wish to be are lands where the days are even shorter. So with a heavy heart and a long good-bye to my wife, I'll force myself out the door, scrape ice off my vehicle's window, set its heater on high, and, with a rapidly cooling cup of hot coffee, begin my short seven-mile drive to the office.

On the best mornings, if I am lucky, the sun's first warming rays will be amplified by snow-covered farm fields that brighten the day and help me to fully wake up. By the time I reach Havana, only three miles away, the coffee is gone; so I'll usually stop at one of several convenient stores for another cup before embarking on the final miles to work at the Forbes Biological Station northeast of town. If I have the time, I'll make a detour to the Illinois River and maybe even sit idle for a few minutes, reminiscing about summer canoe trips and hikes at the Emiquon National Wildlife Refuge, which can be seen across the river from Havana's Riverfront Park. It is here that I may see my first bald eagle of the morning, perching quietly in a large tree along the river's edge or flying over the river in search of the day's first meal of fish. There may also be ring-billed gulls and herring gulls. And if the floodplain lakes that flank the river are frozen, there may be common mergansers and common goldeneyes swimming and diving in whatever open water is available. But my time is usually running out, so after only a few quick moments, I'll put my car into gear and head out of town.

My route stays close to the river bluffs, and I'll typically see several more eagles by the time I reach the office. If a wind is blowing from the river, updrafts may form, and eagles will be soaring just over the treetops near the edge of the bluff. Occasionally, conditions will be just right for the wind speed to match an eagle's forward motion, and the bird will be seen hanging motionless in the sky. Upon reaching Quiver Creek, where the biological station is located, I'll listen for calling eagles as my vehicle passes over the levee leading to the parking area. They perch in the trees over the creek, which usually has quite a bit of open water, except during the longest periods of freezing weather. From my office window, it is not unusual to see an eagle fly past or even grab a fish from the water's surface.

I suspect that it would be easy to take such scenes for granted, but I fight that tendency. Because I always try to recall how the majority of Americans living in big cities commute to their jobs: traffic snarls, crowded buses or commuter trains, the pushing crowds. I was once in that situation many years ago, and I have not forgotten. But it is comforting for me to know that many folks who live where I do also appreciate the eagles. And, of course, there are those with no interest at all; but everyone is certainly entitled to their own interests...as I am entitled to mine.

9
The Eagle Quest

Though it was still early morning when I canoed onto the Illinois River, already the coolness of night had evaporated. Branching from the main river, I leisurely paddled down a narrow, winding channel, through a complex of other channels, small lakes, and bottomland forests. The channel led through part of the Sanganois State Fish and Wildlife Area near the confluence of the Sangamon and Illinois rivers. My destination was the site of an active bald eagle nest several miles away.

By late morning I had encountered few people, only a few men in johnboats traveling to their favorite fishing spots. Tree death from recent flood events (several large floods in the 1990s) was very apparent throughout the area. In some places, the forest appeared similar to a late winter scene; almost all of the trees of various species were totally lacking in leaves. The occasional healthy tree (usually a black willow, silver maple, or green ash) stood in stark contrast to the rest. I felt as if I should have been freezing from cold weather rather than perspiring in the heat. In most areas, paddling in the shade was not an option.

The forest, however, was alive with birds in every direction. Cavity-nesting species, in particular, seemed to be doing very well. House wrens and prothonotary warblers were abundant; their songs echoed through the woods. There were also the usual year-round residents such as black-capped chickadees, tufted titmice, white-breasted nuthatches, and the non-native Eurasian tree sparrow. Tree swallows were numerous; they sometimes passed closely by in their search for flying insects, which they had no trouble finding. All of these species, I thought, should benefit from the temporary abundance of standing dead timber (snags).

After passing through a large backwater lake, I picked up the narrow channel again. It led to an area of higher ground where flood-related tree mortality was less. After some distance, I saw a low levee on my right, which partially enclosed the lake with the eagle nest. The lake's water level was somewhat higher than in the channel, and in one place, higher than the levee. So with much difficulty, I maneuvered the canoe into the small cascade, over the levee, and into the lake. Soon I could clearly see the eagle nest tree over a half mile away along the perimeter of the lake.

I paddled slightly closer to the nest tree, and with my binoculars I could make out two immature eagles, each out of the nest and perching on a different branch of the nest tree. I did not approach much closer, though, as a close approach could have caused the birds to fly. I scanned the trees and the sky, but the parents were nowhere in sight. Satisfied that the nest had produced young, I left the quiet backwater lake and followed the Illinois River back to the boat ramp.

Over the next few hours on the main river, I encountered many watercraft including johnboats, a few large pleasure boats, and a towboat pushing several barges. On the weekends, the river becomes much busier. Yet the backwater lake with the eagle nest is relatively inaccessible amid over 10,000 acres of wild floodplain habitat. Hiking to the eagle nest from the river, one would have to fight aggressive mosquitoes, thick tangles of vines growing across piles of fallen timber, poison ivy, and mud. Few probably attempt this. So for this area in Illinois, the eagles could not have chosen a better site to nest.

The eagles, however, built their nest in a dead tree; and many of the larger trees in the area that might be suitable as nest trees were also dead. Eventually, I thought, the nest tree would fall, perhaps not for a few years or maybe during the next wind storm; the eagles would then have to move on and construct a new nest from scratch; though until they did, they would continue to build onto the existing one every year.

Considering this, my first thought was that this should not be cause for concern. Isn't it normal for trees to die and fall? But then I recalled that the recent high tree mortality along the Illinois River is related to artificial modifications of the river's watershed. We are fortunate that Illinois has become a fantastically productive agricultural state with a fine road system and thriving, interesting cities in which to live. But there have been trade-offs: The land can no longer absorb precipitation as it did when wetlands were widespread and streams were in a natural meandering condition. Rather than soaking into the land through wetlands and being slowly delivered to rivers, more precipitation is now more likely to run off the land and be quickly transported through channelized streams to the main rivers, such as the Illinois, which rise in consequence. The Illinois River's floodplain, in addition, has a reduced capacity to store flood waters because levees, in many areas, prevent river floods from spreading across the floodplain; and backwaters connected to the river are largely filled with sediment from erosion on the watershed. As a result of these hydrological changes, the remaining bottomland forests are inundated by floodwaters more often than in the past. Some trees cannot survive such repeated inundation, especially for long periods. So it is very probable that the death of the eagle nest tree is related to these unnaturally frequent and sustained floods. And although many cavity-nesting birds seem to have benefited from an increase in snags, this situation will not last; for all of the standing dead trees will eventually fall, possibly within a short time span.

As I left the river behind, I remembered reading in the book *Eagle's Plume*, by Bruce E. Beans, that habitat loss may possibly be the greatest threat facing bald eagles today. Yet here along the Illinois River—a river that has seen better days—bald eagles still find a few areas suitable for nesting. Something must be right here if successfully nesting bald eagles are present and increasing, as field studies have shown. This point I must remember the next time that floodwaters rise at unusual frequencies or heights or when I look at a floodplain forest site composed mainly of standing dead timber.

* * *

Summer is almost over. Bald eagle nestlings throughout the Midwest have long fledged. Today the river is almost at its lowest level in quite some time. The air holds an unmistakably present yet faint odor of silty mud from recently receded flood waters, a coating of which lines the river banks and covers plants of the forest floor and decaying organic debris. Paddling the canoe in the shallow backwaters is difficult; in some areas, the paddle passes through only a few inches of water, and the bottom of the canoe must be pushed with considerable effort across the soft, silty lake bottom. I pause to rest and watch a migrating osprey, and then notice two large dark birds soaring about in the general direction of the eagle nest. I did not really expect to find either of the two immature eagles seen earlier in the summer, but both of the soaring birds are first-year bald eagles. I watch the birds for a while and continue onward with an uncertain, yet very good, feeling.

10
Wings Over the River:
A Portrait of Illinois' Swallows

The late July heat slowly dissipated as the sun approached the horizon. Above the wide expanse of the Illinois River, the air was filled with swallows. All six species common to Illinois were present, though most were tree and bank swallows. And all were doing the same thing: foraging on the wing for flying insects. I found it difficult to make sense out of the many birds flying in every imaginable direction. The different species seemed all mixed up, each swallow foraging over the river on an independent flight plan. It was an impressive display of life.

Gazing upon this scene, I could not help but reflect on a basic principle of ecology which states that no more than one species can fill exactly the same role or niche in an ecosystem. Yet here were six aerial insectivores, apparently all feeding in the same way, in the same area, on the same food items. This summer's post-breeding spectacle, however, portrayed only one aspect of their lives, probably the portion where the most competition occurs. While all of Illinois' swallow species—tree, northern rough-winged, barn, bank, cliff, and purple martin—may behave in similar ways during some spans of time, I knew that I would have to more closely investigate their behaviors during the breeding season (when the swallows are in Illinois) to see how each species uses the available habitat in a different manner.

Indeed, once the swallows arrive on the breeding grounds from distant overwintering areas, each species begins to diverge rather obviously from the others in habitat choice and behavior. They partition the landscape's resources so that all species may co-exist, reproduce, and provide a new generation for the future. How each type of swallow does this illustrates the concept of niche separation.

Rough-winged and bank swallows nest in burrows in vertical soil exposures such as those found along streams. Rough-wings also nest in other types of holes and crevices. Bank swallows actually excavate their own burrows several feet into the soil and form small to large colonies. It is not certain whether rough-winged swallows excavate their own burrows or always use abandoned burrows of belted kingfishers or bank swallows. Although the rough-wings are the most solitary of the Illinois swallows, sometimes they will place nests on the edge of a bank swallow colony. Here, given this high degree of resource-use overlap, we might expect the more numerous bank swallows to drive out the rough-wings, but both species seem to tolerate each other. Because nest predation is greater near the edge of the colony, perhaps the bank swallows find an overall benefit by having some of the edge nests occupied by rough-wings. But other than not having to excavate their own burrows, how do rough-wings benefit?

There are many disadvantages of nesting in large colonies. One study in Michigan by John L. Hoogland and Paul W. Sherman showed that for different sizes of bank swallow colonies, as colony size increases, there is more competition for nest sites, nest materials, and mates. At larger colonies, there is also an increased chance that parents may not recognize their own still-dependent young after the young aggregate into larger groups with other fledglings. Parents might then expend time and energy to partially raise another pair's young, possibly at the expense of their own. Another disadvantage of colonies is that as colony size increases, fleas and swallow bugs (wood tick-sized, bloodsucking bedbugs) are more easily transmitted among individuals. So again, why should rough-winged swallows accept all of the disadvantages and locate themselves on the edge of a bank swallow colony?

Even though large colonies have many disadvantages to birds, and they can actually attract the attention of predators, colonies are highly effective in predator detection—and defense in some cases (mobbing the predator). While walking along Salt Creek in Logan County one spring, I noticed a bank swallow colony just below the steep drop off of the creek bank. When I was directly above the burrows, the swallows formed themselves into a great whirling cloud that circled directly overhead, with each bird vociferously calling. I am not sure if this tactic could actually repel a determined predator, but it surely kept my attention and caused me to desire an escape. A large bank swallow colony is a chaotic affair, much like a schoolyard full of highly energetic children during recess on the first warm, sunny spring day. If I were a bank swallow, I would probably locate myself as far away as possible from the colony to dig my burrow, and then choose not to breed. But bank swallows seemingly thrive in the chaos.

Cliff swallows are even more highly colonial and social than bank swallows. They build their gourd-shaped nests made of mud on cliffs, on the undersides of bridges, and on buildings. Because of this, cliff swallows are not in competition with bank and rough-winged swallows for nesting sites. Probably because of the use of bridges, cliff swallows have actually been increasing in Illinois. A very large colony, for example, is under the U.S. Route 136 Bridge to Keokuk, Iowa, directly over the Mississippi River. Cliff swallows are so highly social that even what might easily be a solitary activity, such as gathering mud for nest construction, has a social context. Cliff swallows in groups spend less time looking for predators and are more efficient at gathering mud than lone swallows. The cliff swallow colony, in fact, is an integrated unit. Breeding is highly synchronized within the colony, and the colony acts as an information exchange center to the location of food resources. Well-fed individuals are followed by others as they leave the colony en route to known food concentrations. But all of the disadvantages associated with nesting in a colony, such as increased pest transmission, competition for resources, etc. still apply. In fact, the highly social cliff swallows themselves compound the disadvantages. A female may not only lay eggs in another cliff swallow's nest, but may also toss out the host's eggs before physically transferring her own egg to the host's nest.

Nest infestations of fleas and bugs at cliff swallow colonies can defy the imagination: In an intensive, long-term study in Nebraska, Charles R. Brown and Mary Bromberger Brown found as many as 2,500 swallow bugs in some nests. Nestlings in highly infected nests fared worse than those in cleaner nests. Bug infestations can actually be so bad that cliff swallows may not use a colony site every year, presumably to give bug populations a chance to die out.

Although aggregations of barn swallow nests are referred to as colonies, the species is much less social than the bank and cliff swallows. Small colonies may form in appropriate locations, but the birds seem to go about their activities solitarily, rather than exhibiting the social qualities of the tightly knit cliff or bank swallow colonies. Barn swallows, as the name implies, build their bowl-shaped nests constructed of mud pellets mainly on artificial structures such as buildings and bridges. Historically, nesting sites may have been limited to cave entrances and cliffs. So barn swallows, like cliff swallows, have increased with the advance of roads and buildings across the landscape. In nest site selection, barn swallows are now very similar to cliff swallows, and the possibility for competition between the two certainly exists.

Their foraging patterns are slightly different, however. Barn swallows tend to forage low over the ground—following the contours of the landscape—or low over the water. Cliff swallows, in contrast, may fly to considerable heights in close-knit flocks following swarms of insects rising on warm air. This small difference in foraging style may be enough to reduce niche overlap so that both species can better co-exist in the same area. But cliff swallows are more aggressive than barn swallows, and may usurp barn swallow nests at sites where both species occur. And cliff swallows are increasing in Illinois while barn swallow populations appear to be somewhat stable.

Of the Illinois swallow species, the barn swallow is the only one that regularly has two broods in succession. I observed second brooding several times over the last few years at a small barn swallow colony located inside an abandoned boathouse along the Illinois River. I was surprised each year, as some nests contained nestlings in the early stages of development long after other nests and other species of swallows had fledged young. The energy requirements necessary to prepare for a long fall migration to overwintering areas in South America must be great enough, a second brood notwithstanding. But, by locating their nests along the Illinois River, the barn swallows I observed using the boathouse were very fortunate. The river and its backwaters are a prodigious source of insects. Many insect species spend the immature stages of their lives on the bottom of the river and the adjacent floodplain lakes, later emerging in great numbers on hot summer days.

I recall one evening sitting on the sandy bank of the Illinois River opposite the mouth of the Spoon River. Thousands of mayflies had emerged from the river and were hovering as much as 10 to 15 feet above the shore, but not extending very far out over the river. Every once in a while, a fast-flying swallow plowed through the delicate cloud of insects. Also on that evening, and on many other summer evenings before and after, clouds of midges seemed to dance about over the surface of the river. There are always insects over the river. And the swallows take full advantage of this food resource.

Most of the time, though, as I look out over the Illinois River, I see empty air. Yet the swallows can clearly see the many tiny invertebrates flying over the water. The eyes of birds possess several special anatomical features that may enhance visual functions such as peripheral vision and the ability to detect small objects. In addition, color oil droplets within the eyes help to increase contrast. And avian eyes are sensitive to near ultraviolet light, to which humans are blind. Swallows also have their eyes placed forward, rather than on the sides of the head as in most other passerines, giving them binocular vision. When looking out over the Illinois River from a daytime perch, swallows are clearly seeing a lot more than empty air.

Tree swallows, even more than barn swallows, are attracted to the Illinois River valley with its complexity of wetland habitats. A great number of flood-killed trees cover the river's bottomlands, many resulting from the too frequent summer floods of recent decades. Tree swallows nest in dead trees, in holes, and in cavities made by other species such as woodpeckers; they also use artificial nest boxes. This is a major factor in niche separation among tree swallows and bank, cliff, barn, and rough-winged swallows—although rough-wings may occasionally use tree holes. Snags tend to be haphazardly spread across the landscape, causing tree swallows to be rather solitary nesters. In areas where snags are abundant, such as a beaver pond or a flood-killed bottomland forest, tree swallows attempt to nest as far as possible from other tree swallow pairs. A study by Wallace B. Rendell and Raleigh J. Robertson, in Canada, showed that tree swallows set up and defend territories around nest sites where each territory may include several suitable nesting cavities. This behavior actually prevents all possible cavities in an area from being used.

Arriving on the breeding grounds as early as possible is one way to win nest sites, but insectivores must wait for warmer weather when insects are more active. Unlike other swallows, however, tree swallows are able to push their spring arrival slightly earlier by adding berries and seeds to their insect diet. This may give them an added edge in finding the best nest cavities. Tree swallows, on average, also don't need to travel as far from winter ranges to reach Illinois compared to other swallows—with the exception of rough-winged swallows, which may have a similar range. Some tree and rough-winged swallows winter along the Gulf of Mexico, while the other swallow species migrate from as far as South America. Even so, aggressive non-native European starlings and house sparrows, which are here all winter, undoubtedly claim many cavities early in the season.

Competition for cavities occurs among tree swallows and other species. The aggressive house wren is very abundant in floodplain forests along the Illinois River, and probably is a formidable competitor for nesting cavities. Along the lower Illinois River, the non-native Eurasian tree sparrow, a close relative of the house sparrow, is becoming quite abundant. Time will tell how the niche overlap with the aggressive non-native species will eventually play out. But at any rate, over the last few decades in Illinois, the tree swallow already appears to have been in decline.

The purple martin is the largest of Illinois' swallows. Like tree swallows, purple martins historically nested in tree holes or other cavities. Today though, Illinois' purple martins build nests mostly in artificial nest houses (i.e., the familiar martin apartment houses). This would seem to imply that the purple martin is a highly colonial species. But purple martin nests were once distributed over the landscape much like tree swallow nests: in open habitats where mostly scattered, appropriate cavities were found. Undoubtedly, there must have been some competition with tree swallows for cavities, but the martin is much larger than the tree swallow and would have been excluded from using the smaller cavities. Purple martins stand apart from the other swallows in their method of flying. They regularly soar much more than any of the other species. Strangely, even with abundant snags available in the Illinois River valley, purple martins seem to be loyal to nesting in martin houses. Is the ecological niche of purple martins in Illinois now inextricably dependent upon human altruism? Does the fact that purple martins are declining in Illinois portend a future emergency? As I have glanced at the mid-summer, mixed species foraging flocks of swallows over the Illinois River, the few individual purple martins have clearly stood out. With binoculars, I have gladly followed those individual martins, closely—filtering out all of the other more numerous swallow species crossing my field of view—until they disappeared beyond the trees bordering the river. More than other swallows, purple martins depend on us.

Soon after sunrise, during the breeding season, the Illinois River valley is saturated with bird song. And the numerous swallows make no small contribution to the cacophony. As I listen, I conclude that the drive to reproduce must be one of the great forces of nature, a goal of life to be met at all costs. What else besides an irresistible force could cause a bird to go through the trouble each and every year to migrate hundreds or even thousands of miles, set up and defend a territory, choose a mate, build a nest, rear young, return to wintering areas, and then turn around and do it all over again? Why not simply stay in the tropics and remain single and carefree? Choice, apparently, does not seem to be an option. Yearly mortality is such that most species would decline to nothing in short order if so much attention were not narrowly and intensely focused on the reproductive cycle each year. This great reproductive force must be necessary, though it can get out of hand quite easily, with overpopulation and an inevitable crash resulting. There is a lesson here, of course, as there frequently is when observing any aspect of the natural world in great detail, seeking answers to questions generated from simple observations.

II

First Glimpse of the Upper Mississippi River Valley

When I first entered the working world in the 1970s, the time did not seem to be one of limitless opportunities. Looking back today, the mid-1970s seem to have been a wasteland: recession; Watergate, and Vietnam fatigue; good-paying manufacturing jobs apparently on the way out, flipping burgers and frying fries on the way in; gas lines; the Misery Index and Jimmy Carter, with his message that America's best days were behind us.

So at 20 years of age, I was quite depressed; living at home and dulling my brain daily at work running a dirty, noisy paper-cutting machine for a low wage that was not enough for me to live on my own; wasting away the evening on inane television programs, then back the next work day for more dullness, dirt, and noise. The pattern of my life seemed laid out before me in the older middle-aged men working beside me at the paper company: 30-year mortgages for a matchbox-sized home and lot, hearing loss, back pain, job-related injury, retirement. Done. Like young men throughout the ages, I asked myself if there was not more to life. Where was there meaning in this uninspiring routine followed by so many? If there were answers to be found somewhere, I could not find them; but I did know that a new motorcycle would not hurt, and might help matters, at least for a while.

With summer and a one-week vacation from work, I hit the road on my new 1978 750K Honda, carrying along only a small bag of belongings strapped to the back seat, plus a vague notion that the further from Chicago I traveled, the better, less hurried, and less crowded the land would become, and the more wild and pristine everything would be. Of course, I had no real basis for such an idea, and I likely did not even form it in so many words, but the idea equated distance with answers; and I instinctively felt that being in the outdoors surrounded by nature was where I would find contentment, a feeling that had deep roots in my childhood experiences in the Chicago area forest preserves—a priceless gift from my parents, I now know.

Solely based on its place on a highway map, I chose Mississippi Palisades State Park as my destination. I had no idea what a palisade was, but the Mississippi River was at the edge of the state, and the park was at the far northwest corner of the state. *Far enough for now*, I reasoned. Longer trips would come later.

Living most of my life on the tabletop flat lands of Chicago, on a drained wetland in fact, I called any slight rise in the land a "hill." So the Driftless Area of northwestern Illinois (that is, an area missed by the land-flattening glaciers) seemed truly mountainous, and I felt to be very far from home, though it was only about 150 miles. When the highway suddenly dropped in elevation to a flat bottomland, I saw the upper Mississippi River for the first time: a wide expanse of greenish-gray turbid water, floating leaves of vegetation in the backwaters, forested islands and banks; all wild. Yet it was not until I first viewed the river and its flood plain from the cliff tops of the state park that I was most impressed. The information kiosk stated that below me the Upper Mississippi River National Wildlife and Fish Refuge stretched northward for 260 miles along the Mississippi River, from Princeton, Iowa, to Lake Pepin in Minnesota and Wisconsin. With a lazy turkey vulture soaring by at eye level and the late afternoon sun in my eyes, I felt, reality to the contrary, that I was gazing upon a pathless wilderness, with Chicago left far behind in a different world; this was a theme I would return to, mostly with disappointment, many times throughout my life of travels.

At that moment, I wanted to drop everything and hike those forests, canoe the channels and bays, get lost in the wilderness, and forget completely about living at home and being strangled by my life of no direction. Here was something better than I had ever before imagined. I knew, though, that I was unprepared for such journeys, and embarking unprepared on an aimless trek through the "wilderness" would have been folly. So I made a mental note to return one day; it was clear that I first needed to find a way to escape the quicksand of the lifestyle I was being pulled down into with each passing year. I needed a plan, and I would return. There would be no Misery Index for me.

Side Channels

Mississippi Palisades State Park, Illinois

12

A Lesson in Nature's Dynamics:
Barton-Sommer's Woodland

The transition is subtle as County Road 3900E, in southeastern Mason County, Illinois, passes through gently undulating upland landscape to the flat bottomlands that border Salt Creek. Dominated by corn and soybean fields and neatly mowed roadsides, modern agriculture has made much of Illinois look uniform. Yet I know that somewhere in the line of trees ahead, along the creek, a little patch of floodplain (52 acres) is different from the rest—a patch spared from development. It is called Barton-Sommer's Woodland, now protected forever by state law as a dedicated Illinois Nature Preserve. Forget shopping malls, Six Flags, and gambling boats on the big rivers. Natural areas are the places I seek out, to think about what Illinois was like two hundred or more years ago, before it was so greatly altered—places to gain insight into the workings of the natural world.

Reading the Land

The dirt road that leads from the county road to Barton-Sommer's

Woodland continues to gradually drop in elevation as it passes through many acres of highly productive farmland. At the preserve border, the vegetation changes abruptly. The old-growth character of the preserve is immediately obvious, especially after I enter the woods: within sight there are a few large standing dead trees; large fallen logs, with pits in the ground where the trees once stood; large decayed logs almost blending completely with the soil; and of course, the enormous bur oaks, sycamore, and some old black walnut and swamp white oak trees. Many of the sycamores lean at what seem to be precariously low angles, sunken into the soft, moist alluvial soil, and yet they stand solidly (this I hope as I walk beneath an old leaning giant with a diameter of about four feet).

The bur oaks appear as battered survivors of a lost world, with craggy limbs, exhibiting scars from storm injuries long ago. For many decades, the old trees have survived fires, windstorms, disease, insect infestations, climate change, floods, and other natural adversities. Needless to say, they have also survived being cleared for other land uses—just barely.

There are no trails at this preserve, so I walk in a southerly direction in order to eventually intersect with Salt Creek. It is not long before I discover that walking here on a mid-summer day requires extra patience: the ground flora is dominated in most places by a dense cover of wood nettles interspersed with Virginia wild rye. The nettles create a nearly unbroken canopy about three feet above the ground, which makes it difficult to see the many obstacles hidden on the forest floor. The canopy of nettles is even more effective at obscuring the ground because the nettles' leaves arrange themselves to minimize self-shading. Harvestman spiders use these plants extensively, and many can be seen gingerly stepping from one leaf to another. I, too, walk carefully among the nettles, since they harbor minute syringe-like hairs that penetrate the skin on contact and inject an irritating chemical that causes itching and swelling. Tripping and falling into them would not be a pleasant experience.

Beneath a large bur oak is a place relatively clear of vegetation. I sit below a tree to listen to a singing wood thrush and watch a bluebird enter an old woodpecker cavity in a standing dead tree, much decayed and about ready to fall. Nearby a barred owl calls, perhaps reacting to my intrusion. House wrens are extremely abundant; their songs dominate the early morning breeding bird chorus. Judging from other bottomland woodlands I have visited along the Illinois River, I expect to see many red-headed woodpeckers; but, curiously, despite my many visits to this preserve over the last two years, I have only seen red-headed woodpeckers here a few times. Downy and red-bellied woodpeckers and northern flickers are common. Later I see a pileated woodpecker, which emits a piercingly loud call when our eyes meet.

The tree that I lean against is perched at the edge of a steep drop off that plunges several feet. Beyond the drop off, most of the trees are young silver maples. I see no large patriarchical bur oaks, and I think that this must be a young forest. In fact, after walking along the edge of the drop off, it becomes clear that this lower area is an old meander bend of Salt Creek, abandoned by the stream many years ago. Though this area is dry, I can tell from accumulations of debris and the dominance of the flood-tolerant silver maples that every once in a while the abandoned channel reconnects with the creek, and the old channel again holds water. Perched on the outside edge of the meander bend, the bur oak that I sit under had actually been saved from eventually toppling into the creek when the main channel became diverted and the meander bend stopped moving toward the oak.

Elsewhere in the preserve, there is more evidence of previously shifting stream channels: curved undulations of the ground that fit together like a giant jigsaw puzzle. The meander scars in the ground show that over the long-term, the floodplain is a dynamic environment, altering its shape as the stream slowly moves across the land. It is as natural and inevitable as the earth turning on its axis, as rain falling from the sky, just as water seeks its level. Yet barring catastrophic events, a stream alters its path across the land very gradually, unlikely to really be noticed by anyone over the short-term of a few years. The abandoned channels at Barton-Sommer's Woodland provide a lesson in perspective: in nature, change is often gradual and continuous over long periods of time, and rather difficult to perceive over the short-term.

Though the flowing stream is continually changing the very ground of the riparian woodland, I find no hint of this power in the perfectly clear, shallow water gently flowing over the sandy creek bottom. It is hard to imagine this to be the same stream that during the voluminous spring rains, only a few months before, boiled past with power, turbulence, and turbidity. Where, I thought, did the fish go during the high, fast flows? They must have found slack water refuges. Some were probably carried downstream. The creek is never the same. Standing on part of the dry creek bed at the water's edge I can see leaves being carried downstream under water, bouncing away to eventually break apart into smaller and smaller fragments or become lodged in leaf packs within fallen branches or in quiet pools. Immature stages of aquatic insects will feed upon the decaying leaves; some of the insects will become food for fish, while others will eventually change to adults and fly over the water to become a meal for foraging birds and bats. The stream provides a good open area for foraging flycatchers, kingfishers, and swallows. Bank swallows and northern rough-winged swallows build their nests into the vertical stream banks. But when the water is high, many habitats may be eliminated; the swallows may be flooded out; shorebirds looking for mudflats will have to fly onward; great blue herons seeking to catch fish in shallow, clear water pools will have to look elsewhere.

I have grown accustomed to the surprises offered by the stream, never quite knowing what to expect. But in the old growth woodlands, I expect stability, almost a given changelessness. On every visit to this preserve, I look forward to following a regular path through the woods from one favorite tree to another. Yet is this a realistic expectation? Or does it only seem that way because of my limited abilities to notice gradual change or to read the text written within the woods themselves?

Disturbance is the Rule

I cannot help but be fascinated by the old bur oaks. At times I have stared into their crowns as if expecting some sort of answer to materialize as to what is actually happening around me. The fact that the trees will surely die and fall at some time is no great revelation. But what will happen after the old trees fall? In the past, they undoubtedly were replaced by other bur oaks. Yet I have searched for evidence of oak regeneration many times, and have managed to find only a few small, widely-spaced seedlings and understory trees—not much to replace the current generation. There are many young hackberries, elms, and bitternut hickories, but few young oaks. The woodland understory and subcanopy are also lacking in oaks. So when one of the elderly oaks finally does fall and die, it is likely to be replaced in the canopy by a hackberry or one of the other species common in the understory. If this situation were to continue, Barton-Sommer's Woodland may likely look very different in the future, more altered than it has already become from times past.

The land surveyors of Mason County in the early 1800s described the area around Barton-Sommer's Woodland as an open woodland, wet prairie, and prairie with only a few scattered trees (i.e., savanna). It was an environment with abundant light and little shade, perfect for the regeneration of oak trees. And the main factor that kept it that way was fire. Fire during drought years was even more effective.

So the floodplains burned; the oak woodlands and wet prairies, when they were dried out, burned. Fires could have been started by lightning, but most were probably set by Native Americans to keep the woodlands open, to maintain the prairies, and to improve forage for grazing mammals, which they hunted. The resulting environments favored the fire-tolerant oaks over other species, except in areas where the fires could rarely reach. Shade-tolerant plants must have been scarce. A bur oak savanna or woodland is a fire-disturbance-dependent natural community.

While the Native Americans and fire have not been influential factors at Barton-Sommer's Woodland for many years, grazing livestock seemed to have prevented many trees from becoming established, and the area retained its open, savanna-like character. Then, as grazing was eliminated around the 1930s, for whatever reason, the open woods began to gradually change as imperceptibly as a meandering stream. The evidence of change and periodic disturbance, though, is manifested in the woodland itself and in the contours of the soil. Nature is dynamic; there can be no doubt.

A Prescription for the Future

The future of Barton-Sommer's Woodland is now in the hands of state biologists. And processes that helped create and maintain the open woodland and savanna will be re-introduced. As the Native Americans had done for millennia, biologists will periodically burn the woods, to suppress the intolerant species and to help maintain an open character to the forest. A master plan for management includes opening up the canopy to increase light levels in order to encourage oak regeneration and bringing in seeds of prairie and savanna plants from nearby natural areas to restore the plant community to a state similar to what it had been like over two hundred years ago and beyond. Bluebirds and red-headed woodpeckers, and other remaining species that once thrived in the original savannas of Illinois, will benefit from the savanna restoration.

When visiting the old-growth woodlands, I have always felt a sense of stepping back in time hundreds of years, as if the experience were not

A Lesson in Nature's Dynamics: Barton-Sommer's Woodland

quite in keeping with the rest of the world around me; as if the woods and I were both anachronisms. At Barton-Sommer's Woodland, that fanciful feeling is now obscured by knowledge of how the area has changed in only a few decades, even though it has remained relatively "untouched" throughout that short time span. Years from now, after the savanna has become re-established, after many hours of hard work and patience by restorationists, perhaps the feeling of timelessness will return.

As I follow the county road out of the bottomlands, I cannot help but reflect on what real impact a 52-acre preserve can have on the overwhelmingly larger surrounding cultural landscape. Fifty-two acres is pretty small. Yet even though most of Illinois' natural areas are small and separated from each other, I am convinced that they are all worth saving and restoring. Because even though it is likely our natural areas will remain small and fragmented (we must be realistic), perhaps one day we may have a chance to reconnect these fragments.

Side Channels

13

Dead Trees, Disturbance, and Illinois' Red-headed Woodpeckers

The Illinois River at Two Rivers National Wildlife Refuge was over its banks in a typical spring flood. I canoed through the forest about a foot above ground. Filtered sunlight gave the woods an almost phosphorescent light green glow; humidity was low, mosquitoes absent. These were perfect conditions to simply sit and listen to the discordant croakings and other bizarre sounds coming from the great blue heron rookery above my head.

Then, just when the thought struck that I was within the wildest, most primeval place in Illinois, where natural rhythms of the river reign supreme, the strangest growling sound of all commanded my attention. The sound came not from herons, but from two red-headed woodpeckers vying for a coveted hole near the top of a standing dead tree. Although red-headed woodpeckers are abundant along the river, and on that day all seemed right, in fact, the red-headed woodpecker has been declining in Illinois by nearly 2 percent per year. I was not sure, but I suspected perhaps the decline might have something to do with most of Illinois being just about the opposite of wild and primeval. In effect, the woodpeckers delivered an environmental message to me that I found troubling. I felt compelled to begin a search for more information.

Habitats

One of the most unusual behaviors one would expect a woodpecker to engage in is flycatching for insects. Woodpeckers are experts at climbing trees. In general, though, they appear much less agile in flight compared to tyrant flycatchers or any of the swallows. Yet leaving a foraging perch to pick out an insect from the air, sometimes after a convoluted chase, is a common foraging technique for red-headed woodpeckers during the breeding season. This type of behavior requires open habitats with widely-spaced trees. Indeed, the cavity-nesting red-headed woodpecker is often characterized as a bird of savannas, a transitional habitat type between true prairie (totally lacking in trees) and closed-canopy forest. But since most of Illinois' savannas have long been replaced with developed landscapes, breeding red-heads have adapted to other types of open landscapes, including farm country, which serve as surrogates for the missing savannas. I have often observed red-heads flying across agricultural fields, eventually landing on a wooden utility pole, flying from pole to pole, and hawking for insects over the fields and roads. In some instances, they may return after a catch to the original foraging perch. Perhaps the utility poles form the same function as scattered standing dead timber in their original savanna habitats.

Hawking red-heads can also be found along Illinois' rivers, lakes, and wetlands. Floodplain woodlands along the Illinois River, in particular, appear to provide ideal breeding habitat. The floodplain woodlands have suffered greatly in recent years from frequent flooding. But this has given rise to an abundance of snags and has caused most floodplain woodlands to have a rather open aspect.

And, of course, nesting sites must be easy to locate in the open floodplain woodlands, given the great abundance of large snags and large living trees with dead limbs. Even logs lying and decaying upon the forest floor enhance foraging opportunities, as decaying timber normally harbors an abundance of insect life. Dead wood, without a doubt, is an important habitat feature of living woodlands. In fact, red-headed woodpeckers may even be absent from wooded areas lacking snags. And given a choice, red-heads may actually prefer to forage on dead rather than live trees.

Oak snags are particularly valuable to wildlife because they tend to last longer than snags of other tree species. Larger specimens last the longest. In addition, the furrowed bark of oaks provides a larger surface area for insects to hide compared with smooth-barked species such as maple. Oaks also produce nutritious mast in the form of acorns. And, for overwintering red-headed woodpeckers, abundant mast is an absolute necessity.

Yet not all oak-hickory woodlands and forests produce abundant fruit every year. Mast years, when many individual oak trees within the same area produce a great number of acorns all at the same time, typically occur only every two to five years. Moreover, species in the red oak group (black, blackjack, pin, red) require 18 months to produce an acorn, compared with six to eight months for species in the white oak group (bur, post, white). To complicate the situation even further, mast years appear to be induced by a variety of unpredictable, interacting environmental factors such as temperature regime, light duration and intensity, and nutrient and water availability. The end result is that, from year to year, a good mast crop is unreliable.

Red-headed woodpeckers have adapted to this unreliability by evolving migratory behavior. Other species of woodpeckers, such as the downy and red-bellied, may overwinter in their breeding territories. If mast is not available, though, red-heads will migrate after the breeding season. I have readily observed this phenomenon in the floodplain woodlands along the

Illinois River—which usually are dominated by silver maple, green ash, and cottonwood—because these areas tend to have a high density of red-headed woodpeckers in the summer, but lack the species during the fall and winter. Many red-heads move south to the comparatively heavily forested parts of southern Illinois, which has a higher density of overwintering red-heads than the rest of the state. Others find sites with heavy acorn crops in smaller wooded areas. During winter, red-heads may occupy forests that are much less open than their breeding habitats, because insects are mostly inactive, and the hawking foraging strategy is seldom used.

How soon red-headed woodpeckers detect a mast year in progress is unknown. But by late fall, they begin to enter one of two major phases of winter behavior. The first phase involves claiming and defending small territories, one per bird, and storing acorns within their territories. (Although acorns are without a doubt the most important mast used by red-headed woodpeckers, they have been known to store beechnuts, pecans, and even grasshoppers.)

Sand Prairie-Scrub Oak Nature Preserve (1,460 acres) is about three miles east of the small Illinois River town of Bath in Mason County. The woodlands and savannas of the preserve are dominated by black oak and blackjack oak (plus hybrids of the two species). The open woodlands provide good red-head habitat for breeding as well as overwintering. During some winters, red-heads appear to be completely absent. Then, in other years, they seem to be the most common overwintering woodpecker species in the preserve. During mast years, I have sometimes heard their "quirr" calls from throughout most of the preserve's woodlands. Their territories appear to be quite small; and, because the woods are open with little underbrush, sometimes from a single vantage point it is possible to see two or three individuals in different territories. Studies at other sites documented territory sizes to be from about one tenth of an acre to five acres. Territory size is apparently flexible in order to respond to the amount of mast available; that is, during poor acorn production years, larger territories would be necessary, and conversely.

Red-headed woodpeckers use snags to store acorns and other mast. After their initial caches are complete, the red-heads enter the second phase of winter behavior. This consists of long periods of quiet time perching, and time spent defending their territories and restoring their caches of acorns. The birds apparently move some of their acorns to other caches in accordance with the well-known adage of not keeping all of one's eggs in one basket. Even with a strategy of aggressive territorial defense, where a single red-head will drive off any bird that it perceives to be a competitor (blue jay, tufted titmouse, white-breasted nuthatch, or red-bellied woodpecker), piracy is common. Sometimes red-headed woodpeckers may even cover their acorn store with slivers of wood torn from snags. If the slivers are slightly damp, they will form a nice seal upon drying. Another tactic for protecting acorn supplies is to hammer the acorns into the deep furrows of oak trees, which few birds are able to remove.

Sand Prairie-Scrub Oak Nature Preserve is another of those rare and diminishing areas in Illinois still wild enough to give a sense of the original Illinois landscape. Frequent fires (actually controlled burns) have left their mark on the landscape. Ultimately, and taken to the extreme, fire favors grassland over trees. Though black and blackjack oaks at the preserve have thick bark and are fairly fire resistant, they are not totally immune from damage. And if a collection of fallen branches, twigs, and leaves has gathered at the base of a tree, a hot fire can do extensive damage. Eventually, a fire-damaged tree will have fire scars, where fungi and bacteria can enter, and dead branches and dead wood within the trunk where parts of the tree can break off during strong winds. But like the standing dead timber in the Illinois River's floodplain woodlands, snags and fire-damaged trees in these upland oak woodlands play a necessary role in maintaining the ecological health of the system as a whole. There may even be an equilibrium established whereby snags are lost to decay at about the same rate at which they are created by natural processes, such as fire and disease.

I once stood at Sand Prairie-Scrub Oak Nature Preserve over the faint, lightly tinted image of a log in charred dust—all that was left of the log following a fire of major proportions. The image suggested that even within this complex mix of destruction, ecological balance, and rebirth, the red-headed woodpecker has made a home for thousands of years. It was so unlike the modern human relationship with the natural landscape, where we are like uninvited guests who disrupt our host's normal routines, overstay our welcome, and have no intention of leaving. And so, now it is necessary for all of us to find a way to live together.

Problems

As I have watched red-headed woodpeckers purposely flying across farm fields, their wings flashing in characteristic black and white, they have seemed little interested in the straight rows of corn and soybeans and neatly mowed roadsides. To be sure, people all over the world have benefitted from crops produced on our modern farms, which are impressive and efficient business operations deserving of admiration; but there have been some negative side effects. In recent years, farm sizes have increased, and many owners seem to find little incentive to keep windbreak tree lines along the former property boundaries. The resulting intensively row-cropped landscape with few trees is poor habitat for red-headed woodpeckers. In most cases, the windbreaks are the only hint of semi-wild habitat in an otherwise tamed and broken landscape. Although most of Illinois has been domesticated for quite some time, the pace of natural habitat loss has increased even more within the last half century.

For decades urban areas have been sprawling outward with an accelerating rapidity, despite small gains in human populations in most cases. For example, between 1970 and 1990, population gains in the Chicago metropolitan area were minimal, but suburban sprawl, and all that the term implies, expanded by 45 to 65 percent. And where we find low-density subdivisions and isolated estates—outposts of future sprawl—we find neatly manicured lawns, trimmed shrubbery, and artificial landscaping, with nary a native plant in sight. Would a standing dead tree or rotting log on one's lawn seem appropriate for this picture? Of course, I would say without hesitation. But most in our society would emphatically answer: absolutely not! And so we find suburban developments as they are. Snag-less suburban sprawl cannot be good for red-headed woodpeckers, given the fact that dead trees are such an important component of their habitats throughout the year.

Because of the red-headed woodpecker's affinity for roadside poles and hawking for insects over roads, the species probably has a higher chance than most woodpeckers at colliding with vehicles. But although this idea seems logical, results from limited studies have not been conclusive. Even so, with more vehicles on more roads each year, and with miles driven per vehicle increasing, it would seem surprising, indeed, if there were not an increasing number of collisions with red-headed woodpeckers.

The proliferation of the non-native cavity-nesting European starling in all habitats across Illinois has frequently been cited as a cause for population declines of many bird species, including the eastern bluebird and red-headed woodpecker. But it may be that because breeding of starlings and red-heads are not synchronized (starlings begin nesting earlier than red-heads), and red-heads are actually more aggressive at nest hole defense than starlings, red-heads can probably co-exist with starlings, all else being equal.

However, "all else" is far from equal. A much more intractable problem lies at the heart of the way nature works and the natural processes that have been either stymied or highly altered. For thousands of years, fire at varying intensities and frequencies was a dominant disturbance factor influencing whether this or that tract of land grew prairie, forest, or the transitional savannas. Furthermore, the oak savannas and woodlands are actually maintained by fires; they require fire to merely exist. The fire-resistant bark of oaks even attests to this. Without at least an occasional fire, savannas and open woodlands soon grow a denser understory, where oak seedlings are shaded out, eventually giving rise to a dense, closed-canopy forest lacking an oak component. It is common today in many of Illinois' remaining old-growth woodlands to see large, old, healthy, mast-producing oaks in the canopy, while the understory and seedling layers are typically lacking in oaks; that is, lacking in future generations, despite the still-abundant acorn crops. In many oak woodlands, fire-intolerant sugar maple saplings are standing ready, by the hundreds, to compete for the canopy when the oaks eventually fall.

Although prescribed fires are regularly set by resource managers at some locations to reverse this widespread trend, it is unclear whether these tame, controlled fires are enough to maintain the oak communities. Most prescribed fires are probably not even close to the landscape-scale conflagrations of the past that actually created the savannas. And with insurance companies and lawyers increasingly becoming part of the discussion, it is getting more difficult to plan and carry out controlled fires. In the end, if we lose our oak woodlands in Illinois, overwintering red-headed woodpeckers, dependent upon mast crops as they are, will have to migrate elsewhere. Breeding pairs, though, will probably still find a home along the Illinois River and other major streams.

Challenges

I think it is safe to say that Illinois will never again be wild and primeval, although many small, protected natural areas remain. I can travel to the Illinois River valley and spend a few hours watching great blue herons, or forget about modern society completely within the wilds of Sand Prairie-Scrub Oak Nature Preserve, where fire is still a dominant disturbance. But when I see a red-headed woodpecker, the message is clear that today all of us face many environmental challenges. Perhaps someday, if we rise to these challenges, the bird may deliver a different message.

Side Channels

Snags along the Upper Mississippi River, Iowa

14

From the Misery Index to Havana

As my motorcycle and I bounced along the tollway at 55 miles per hour, the blowing air did little to lessen effects of the mid-July heat, humidity, and intense solar radiation. I was heading back home to the flat urbanity of Chicagoland from the spacious, verdant views of northwestern Illinois and the Mississippi River. It was 1978, and I was traveling from where I preferred to be to a place I wished to escape from. The grand view of the upper Mississippi River at Palisades State Park stayed with me all the way; but as I exited the Eisenhower Expressway at Harlem Avenue, my immediate concern was pizza and beer; while on the periphery of thought, questions not present at the beginning of the trip nagged. Though today I hesitate to say that that trip changed my life's direction, it did spawn a series of questions about where my life was heading at the time, and how I might seize control.

Throughout high school, I not only simply appeared to be disinterested in learning, as a typical student strives to be viewed among classmates; my disinterest was quite genuine. And so, those four years were mostly wasted. Yet even with my diploma and high-school attitude a mere three years old in 1978, I knew and could not escape the knowledge that the reins to control my life could only be found in education. My teachers were right after all. So by the fall of the year, I began making plans to rebuild the skills I had lost since my good-student days of primary school, and then to begin a formal education that would lead away from the dead ends.

But despite the aftereffects of the Mississippi River trip and a lifetime of being drawn to wild places, it never seemed to have occurred to me that a fine career could be had in nature-related employment. There was no doubt that education was the answer, but what field was I to pursue? What I did know was that I was not fit for a professional career in business, with its suits, neat hair, and clean shaven faces, possessing as I did a Holden Caulfield-like disdain for phoniness, which I imagined permeated the world of business as much or more than politics. The healthcare profession was not even an option. And I mostly lacked the hands-on abilities and horse sense necessary for a skilled trade such as carpentry or auto mechanics.

While sorting this out over a few years, with time served in academia and industry, a curious change had fallen over me: I began reading widely and was developing an almost insatiable curiosity concerning just about everything, which increasingly included the natural world, and a desire for knowledge for its own sake—the "desire to know." This from one who, as a high school student, had skipped classes and once turned in a five-page report on five-by-seven-inch sheets of paper, with wide margins, hoping the teacher would not notice (no such luck). And, more importantly, I was returning to an early fascination with nature and wild areas. Before too long I wanted to know more about all aspects of the natural world, and I began to revisit the forest preserves of my youth.

One fall day in the early 1980s, during this period of sorting out where I belonged, I took a long, careful look at some of the common forest birds, the first time I had ever made the effort to do such a thing. Black-capped chickadee, northern flicker, golden-crowned kinglet, downy woodpecker. The diversity of shapes, colors, and behaviors captured my attentions and somehow filled a vague void deep within; I have never forgotten that fall hike in the Cook County forest preserves. Living birds in natural habitats provided an inspiration, orders of magnitude greater than any of our products of industry—computers, space shuttles, tall buildings, large bridges, and other marvels notwithstanding. After several seasons pursuing birds in the forest preserves, combined with an inescapable awareness of the challenges involved in protecting and managing natural resources in Illinois, and flavored with the works of authors such as John Muir, Edwin Way Teale, Sigurd Olsen, and Edward Abbey, I sensed another shift was about to occur in my life.

About this same time, I stumbled upon a magazine advertisement by Cornell University's Laboratory of Ornithology, and I enthusiastically became a member. Their magazine, *Living Bird,* effectively closed the gap for me between the recreational pursuit of birds, mainly for aesthetic appreciation, and scientific inquiry. Before too long I was counting birds and taking note of habitat associations and threats to both, and I began to view my outdoor pursuits in a new light: that of preparing myself to pursue additional education, so that I could, if at all possible, eventually obtain gainful employment in field ecology and habitat protection—if, I hoped, such employment opportunities even existed. Realistically, though, I expected to be disappointed, but I also knew that I had to make an attempt, which ultimately led me to Southern Illinois University at Edwardsville.

One day, lost in thought on the way to one of my final environmental science classes, I paused at the Department of Biological Sciences' bulletin board, which sometimes had job announcements posted. I glanced at the board in a rather offhanded manner when a posting for a biological field technician with the Illinois Natural History Survey (INHS) caught my eye. The position as described would require long hours (okay), extreme conditions (I was still young), and marginal pay (of course), and would involve working on a fish population sampling project on the Illinois River. It would not involve birds and their habitats, though that would eventually come; but I had to start somewhere, and it was more important to seize the opportunity. Fish are actually quite interesting, and the prospect of becoming very familiar with the Illinois River appealed to my sense of adventure. So, of course, I submitted a letter of application immediately, but was fully prepared to ride out the rather poor economic conditions of the early 1990s completing more biology courses at the university—though I was beginning to be a bit burned out with examinations and memorization marathons.

Then, to my surprise, a few weeks later I was invited to a job interview at the INHS field station at Havana, a small Illinois River town. The interview went well, and I was optimistic. And when the good news telephone call eventually came, I was both excited and strangely intimidated. This new position would be the realization of a life trajectory set in motion either on or soon after that thought-provoking motorcycle trip 13 years before, when I passed through the attractive small towns of northwestern Illinois and viewed the upper Mississippi River for the first time. And after I accepted the position, it did not escape my notice that few folks are likely to have a chance to truly realize a dream that once might have seemed quite improbable; I felt about to finally arrive where I should have been in the first place. The convergence of circumstances that eventually led me to Havana, I could not have set up better myself.

15

The Shorebirds Among Us

They enrich our lives, and the webs of migration that they spin around the world tell us about global connections, global causality, and global responsibility.
–from Handbook of the Birds of the World, Volume 3, by T. Piersma

By late July, the Illinois River's water level had finally dropped to its usual summer low point, and new mudflats were fully exposed. With vegetation not yet having much time to grow, the bare mud attracted hundreds of foraging shorebirds of several species. So I took advantage of the morning shade to survey the birds, intent upon a positive identification of each and every "peep" sandpiper. Birdsong reverberated from throughout the riparian woodlands, and the gentle breezes carried a complex of pleasant scents as dew evaporated from the surrounding vegetation. Then, as I looked away from the shorebirds for a moment to scan for other birds, one of the shorebirds suddenly shattered the peace with the most bloodcurdling scream of terror I had ever heard. In a flash, the shorebirds were all in flight, expertly eluding an attacking peregrine falcon. In a few seconds they were gone, yet I knew that with the "fall" migration fully engaged, this small mudflat, what many folks would consider a mere wasteland, would soon again be a shorebird hotspot.

Of the 319 bird species that can regularly be found in Illinois, 37 are collectively referred to as "shorebirds," and categorized into three families: stilts and avocets; plovers; and sandpipers, snipes, and phalaropes. Only the black-necked stilt, killdeer, spotted sandpiper, upland sandpiper, Wilson's snipe, and American woodcock, however, nest in Illinois; the rest simply migrate through Illinois between overwintering and breeding habitats. The pectoral sandpiper, as a typical example, travels from as far away as southern Argentina to breed within the far reaches of northern Canada above the Arctic Circle. It is maybe not much of an exaggeration to suggest that such a bird has probably seen more of the world in one year of its intense life than most folks are likely to see over a lifetime.

Yet even given the obvious perils faced over their migratory journeys—such as volatile weather, stealthy predators, disturbance by humans, and hostile environments—the benefits surely outweigh the risks, otherwise migratory behavior would not have evolved. Species traveling to the high Arctic, for example, do so to exploit the rich insect life that occurs on the tundra just when young shorebirds hatch and require a constant stream of energy for growth. They also need the insect prey to fuel their own migrations southward before the onset of fall.

During migration, finding the appropriate habitat throughout the journey is a necessity. Along ocean coasts, the tides bring an accurate regularity to dynamic habitats, and good sites are used year after year without fail. The most famous example is probably the Delaware Bayshore on the Atlantic coast, where a variety of shorebirds gorge on the eggs of horseshoe crabs. Both the crab egg laying and peak of shorebird migration occur at the same time in the spring, and this is not a coincidence.

However, at inland sites such as Illinois, the availability of good shorebird habitat is much less reliable. Droughts occur, and wetlands can dry out as in 1988; or habitats can be inundated by torrential floodwaters such as during the Great Flood of 1993. In addition, about 90 percent of Illinois' original wetland habitats have been drained and converted to agriculture, roadways, and urban areas. Shallow-water and mudflat habitats, free of dense vegetation and rich in the small invertebrate life needed by migrating shorebirds, are now few and far between within the modern Midwestern landscape. If high-quality wetlands are not available in spring, sometimes shorebirds can be found in wet agricultural fields, foraging among the previous year's crop stubble. Migrating shorebirds can even be found at sewage treatment lagoons, which tend to support an abundance of invertebrate prey. But even though they have evolved an opportunistic strategy in selecting stopover areas, if appropriate habitats cannot be found, most must simply pass right over Illinois in search of habitats elsewhere.

The Illinois River valley is notable because of its location along the Mississippi Flyway (a term originally applied to waterfowl migrations) and the fact that many areas on the river bottoms are managed in such a way, deliberate or not, that may benefit shorebirds. Chautauqua National Wildlife Refuge is the outstanding Illinois River site, just upriver of Havana. Here, an elaborate system of levees and water-control structures allow refuge staff to manage water levels so that a range of habitat conditions exist (e.g., mudflat, shallow water, dry exposures) to provide for the needs of a variety of shorebird species. The levees also buffer the refuge's wetland plant communities and mudflats from the unpredictable flooding which has been associated with the Illinois River. Though large spring floods typically pour over the refuge's levees nearly every year—inundating shorebird habitats with deep, muddy water—in early summer, the water level is deliberately lowered to expose mudflats. This management scenario mimics the river's natural hydrological cycle, which occurred before the river and its watershed became highly altered by human activities (e.g., navigation lock and dam system). By the middle of July, the post-breeding-season shorebird migration is fully underway. And if all goes well with the river's water levels (i.e., anomalous summer flood waters do not overtop the levees) and before the wetland vegetation has grown too dense, Chautauqua Refuge becomes a shorebird magnet, well into September.

Observation decks at Chautauqua Refuge's Eagle Bluff Access and along the Chautauqua Nature Trail allow for some of the best shorebird viewing anywhere. Mornings provide the optimal viewing conditions with the sun shining from behind or off to the side and with the viewing platforms covered in cool shade. At such times, in my opinion, there is little reason to travel further for excellent shorebird viewing. Of course, not everyone would agree; more highly motivated birders can sometimes be seen roaming the refuge, suffering under the unrelenting solar heat, and slogging through the mud and cockleburs in search of rare birds. Their strenuous efforts, so I later learn, are rarely in vain. Unusual species have included the ruff, red-necked phalarope, red phalarope, and buff-breasted sandpiper.

Some observers are intimidated by shorebird identification because many species have similar shapes and plumage characteristics. A typical experience is to have a "peep" sandpiper, of which there are several nearly identical species, within a clear view and with the sun at a perfect angle, only to end up repeatedly looking back and forth between the field guide and the bird. Sometimes the birds almost seem to be taunting the observers to obtain a positive identification, foraging intently for quite a long time before eventually flying off and leaving the observer in a wake of frustration. Other species, such as the American avocet, are so unique, even the least experienced observer will have success in obtaining an easy identification.

The observation decks at Chautauqua Refuge provide an excellent situation from which to patiently dissect the finer points of shorebird identification, even though the birds may sometimes be quite far away. This same vantage point also allows one to view a great part of the refuge as a whole and to leisurely study shorebird behavior. During the peak of migration, one may easily see many various-sized flocks of shorebirds arriving and departing in what appears to be a confusion of highly coordinated meanderings. Questions quickly arise as to what factors may have caused them to take flight all at one instant in time, or if there are any discernable patterns in their movements and distributions.

One may see species, such as the killdeer, standing upright, functioning as sentinels for signs of danger, and sounding their alarms at the slightest provocation. At the same time, species such as the stilt sandpiper probe for food items with their heads down much of the time, apparently relying upon the sentinels to detect danger. The habitat mosaic in view from Chautauqua Refuge's elevated observation decks includes a variety of water depths along with wet and dry areas. So it is possible, in a single view, to see the various species segregated by small habitat differences.

Shorebirds exhibit a great diversity of shapes and sizes, and this is directly related to the way in which the different species partition the habitat. For example, avocets forage in deeper water, moving their bills through the water with a scything manner; long-legged species, such as greater yellowlegs, use shallow-water areas; peeps typically use moist mudflat areas with little surface water; and sanderlings prefer sandy beaches. Large plovers, such as the killdeer, tend to forage on dryer ground, individually picking at surface prey items, while dowitchers, with their long bills, can probe deeper within the substrate than many other species. Areas offering only a single habitat type will attract fewer species than a diverse mosaic. But of course, a well-known ecological principal is that habitat diversity is directly related to species diversity.

From evolutionary considerations to recognizing subtle ecological patterns, I find observing shorebirds an inspiration. By those same observations, on the other hand, one is confronted by the facts, which tell of Illinois' great loss of wetlands and disturbing population decreases of many shorebird species. Yet to obsess on the negative would seem to allow little acknowledgment of the natural diversity that still remains, albeit somewhat out of the main view, within the cracks and crevices of the modern landscape. It is here that shorebirds survive among us.

Whether along the edges of watercourses or among Illinois River mudflats exposed by retreating floodwaters, shorebirds, having arrived from far beyond the most distant horizons, still engage in the very same activities that have been witnessed by the ages. Today they bind us to the past and to the rest of the planet, tomorrow to our common future.

16

When Hawks Fly

It was a typical March day, on the backside of a high-pressure system moving over the area from the west. I was standing on a high hill that rose just above the surrounding trees, a few miles east of the Illinois River. At the limit of vision, aided by binoculars, I picked out the mere speck of a bird against the broken cloud cover of the southwestern sky. By its quick wing beats alternating with gliding, I knew this bird, even at a great distance, to be a sharp-shinned hawk. When the bird was directly overhead, my neck and arms ached from the strain of holding the field glasses. But I kept the hawk in sight as long as possible, until it blinked out of view in the northern sky, again at the limit of vision.

Over the last few decades, hawk watching has gained in popularity, and this has helped provide insight into the complexities of bird migration and behavior. Yet as we observe the many ways that these raptors follow age-old routes and also adapt to unpredictable environmental factors such as weather, we gain an appreciation for how our world came to be as it is, and how it may inevitably change.

Side Channels

The Strategies of Flight

Weather conditions would seem to be the most pressing and immediate issue confronting any migrating bird. In Midwestern North America, high barometric pressure systems as large as several states may move from west to east with winds blowing clockwise around a central area. As a high-pressure system moves through an area, winds blow from a northerly direction, and then eventually switch to southerly with lower pressure as the system moves off to the east. Northerly winds, in general, favor fall migrant hawks moving toward the south. During spring, migrants move mostly on southerly winds. This I saw quite easily one April day along the Illinois River, when a strong southerly wind brought in hundreds of broad-winged hawks—as well as ominous-looking storm clouds. Usually, though, few hawks will move during storms, a fact I once verified by standing, perhaps foolishly, for several hours in the rain...observing no hawks.

A phenomenon extremely important to the soaring flight of migrating hawks is the formation of vertical air movements called "thermals." Thermals are formed when the land, which warms the adjacent surface layer of air, absorbs solar energy. The warm air rises in a column and is replaced as fast as it rises by nearby cooler air. A soaring hawk can glide over the rising air, and gain altitude without expending much energy from wing flapping. Though rising air columns will eventually dissipate at heights sometimes exceeding one half mile, a hawk may then glide down to the next thermal on its migrational pathway.

A hawk can soar because its body weight in relation to the area of its wings—a term referred to as "wing loading"—is low. A bird with heavy wing loading, such as a mallard duck, must constantly flap its wings, or it will rapidly lose altitude. A turkey vulture, in contrast, has a very light wing loading, even for a soaring bird, and may seem unsteady while soaring, actually appearing to be buffeted about by the winds. During migration, hawks take advantage of their ability to soar, combined with weather conditions and local landscapes, to minimize energy use.

Migrating hawks probably proceed as a broad front of birds until they encounter an obstacle or guiding line such as a river or shoreline. At such places, they may concentrate in large numbers as each bird responds to the landscape in a similar way, pre-conditioned toward such behavior by inherited traits. For example, as fall migrants in Wisconsin are moving toward the southeast on northwest winds, they encounter the western shore of Lake Michigan. Thermals do not form over water because of the high capacity of water to absorb heat. For this reason, many raptor species are reluctant to cross large bodies of open water. Instead of crossing Lake Michigan, they follow the "leading line" of the lake's shore southward, and then most likely move again as a broad front when south of the lake. At such times, an observer on a hill along the western shore of the lake would have a good chance of counting thousands of hawks. Similar phenomena probably occur all around the Great Lakes. At northeastern Minnesota in the fall, for instance, hawks soaring on thermals moving from the northwest encounter Lake Superior and then travel toward the southwest, rounding the lake at Duluth.

The influence of the Great Lakes on hawk flight paths is similar during spring migration. Raptors moving north through Wisconsin and Michigan on a southwest wind may be concentrated toward the tip of the Keweenaw Peninsula, which extends nearly to the middle of Lake Superior. From the top of Brockway Mountain near the tip of the peninsula, one may see the hawks passing overhead, allegedly on their way toward rounding the peninsula in order to head back southward to the mainland. They most likely then pass around the lake at its eastern or western tip. Although of longer duration, this strategy is evidently safer than attempting to cross the large expanse of the frigid lake, with its unpredictable and sometimes violent weather.

On the other hand, although crossing large bodies of water may not be a preferred strategy for raptors, it certainly occurs to some degree for many species. Those that rely less on soaring flight, such as the falcons, are more likely to cross a large lake than a turkey vulture or rough-legged hawk. In any case, it is likely that many raptors of all kinds die every year from being blown out over the Great Lakes or from attempting a crossing under poor conditions.

Hawks use updrafts (or horizontally moving air deflected upward) in much the same way as thermals. Around the Great Lakes, updrafts may form adjacent to the shoreline as air temperatures over the land exceed those over or near the water, and the wind direction is seaward; that is, warm air moves up and over the cooler air near water. Updrafts also occur when winds blowing over broad floodplains of rivers strike the bluffs that parallel the river valleys. Because the Mississippi River is oriented from north to south, it may present a useful leading line as well as good soaring conditions from bluff updrafts.

Raptors respond to landscape features and weather in a similar way year after year. This predictability helps explain why a distributional pattern occurs, illustrating why migrating hawks may be seen in one given area (river bluff) and not another (open water). When the time dimension is added from observations made over the course of a year, other patterns emerge.

Rhythmic Patterns

The length and timing of the migration period for any particular bird species tend to be fairly consistent from year to year, although variations (mostly due to weather) may occur. Also, there is considerable overlap of when different species of raptors are likely to be seen during migration. The number of hawks moving past a point of reference is low at the beginning of that species' migrational period; it gradually increases over several weeks, and is then followed by a steady decline. A migration rhythm of this type, for example, was documented in Maryland over five fall seasons, where three species accounted for over 75% of all the raptors from September through mid-November. Peak numbers of broad-winged hawks occurred between September 15 and 20, sharp-shinned hawks between October 5 and 10, and red-tailed hawks between October 25 and 30. The times when a majority of the broad-wings and red-tails were present essentially did not overlap. Observations near Lake Ontario in spring showed that the sequence of the three raptors was just about the opposite from the fall: the red-tails were the first to move through in March, and the broad-wings were the last, during the latter part of April.

The pattern of distribution over time for some species is over the course of an entire year rather than a single season. The turkey vulture is a common breeding bird in Illinois, while the bald eagle breeds in lower numbers. Turkey vultures move south of Illinois (except for the far southern tip of the state) for the winter, while more bald eagles move into Illinois from the north and are quite common along the state's larger rivers throughout the winter. For these two species, there is little overlap in the time period when both are present in greatest numbers. One winter, I spent considerable time observing birds at the confluence of the Illinois and Mississippi rivers, where a small island is located just opposite the town of Grafton, Illinois; here, eagles could usually be found perching in trees on the island or soaring over the river bluffs. At about the middle of March, turkey vultures perched on the same trees that held only eagles a few weeks before; and turkey vultures, not eagles, soared over the bluffs. Then, in the fall, as the bald eagles began arriving from the north, turkey vultures gradually departed for the south. And this pattern repeats year after year.

Patterns are also apparent over the course of a single day. A daily rhythm may involve a succession of species from early morning to late afternoon, as observers once documented at Cedar Grove, Wisconsin. Movements for accipiter hawks (sharp-shined) were greatest between 8 and 10 o'clock in the morning, for buteos (red-tailed hawk) between 10 and 11 o'clock, and for falcons between 1 and 2 o'clock in the afternoon. All hawk movements ceased after 6 o'clock in the evening.

But why should different species of hawks initiate their migratory flights at different times? And why should some prefer one part of the day and not another? What is special about these patterns for them to repeat year after year? Counting hawks can discover the patterns very well, but does little to provide for explanations.

Beyond the Count

The daily rhythms of the raptor migrants, in fact, result from an internal migratory "clock," presumably present in all migratory birds. Experiments with caged warblers showed that these birds invariably became restless twice a year, at times that corresponded to their normal migratory period, even with the duration of daylight over the course of time held artificially constant. Because internal rhythms were shown to be inherited, they must be the result of the same process, which has been responsible for the migration phenomenon itself: namely, evolution by the process of natural selection. "Selection" is said to occur as the successful line produces more offspring over the long run than those lacking the specific traits possessed by the successful line.

A consideration of why migration occurs may help shed light on certain specifics of migration, such as timing and choice of flight path. Although theories on why birds migrate are varied, all have one concept in common: the benefits derived from segregating breeding and overwintering areas (that is, more successful reproduction) exceeded the costs (risk of travel) and allowed those individuals possessing migratory tendencies to become more successful. Similarly, the daily and seasonal rhythms observed in the migrating hawks are, without much doubt, the result of successes of countless generations whose migratory strategies worked better than others, and who were in better condition at breeding time than those lacking the successful strategies. With this in mind, hawk watching can mean more than simply counting birds.

When the hawks are flying, moving across the continent along their ancient routes, a high hill along a river valley or lake shore is an appropriate place to be—to temporarily part company with mundane responsibilities, to witness a spectacle as seen throughout the ages. It is a small part of the evolutionary process, aloft among the cloud patterns and shifting winds. So there is deep meaning above, in subtle rhythms among the far-flung soaring raptors.

Side Channels

Mackinaw River at Merwin Savanna Nature Preserve, Illinois

17
Carrying on an Electro-shocking Legacy

The late-night, in-and-out people who lived in the basement efficiency apartments were at it again: constantly coming and going, arguing, playing loud music, and slamming doors. I had lived in Havana only a few short months, working at my new job with the Illinois Natural History Survey (INHS), and was just finishing my first field season as a biologist sampling fish populations along the Illinois River. Though I was no longer enrolled in classes at Southern Illinois University at Edwardsville, I still had my master's thesis to finish, and so I was still in a graduate-student-like state of mind, living a serious life, reading job-related scientific articles on rivers and fish biology most evenings long after work; I was deeply involved with my work and studies and had little tolerance for what I was sure were drug-related activities by an ever-changing cadre of "twenty-somethings" with, it seemed to me, nothing better to do with their lives than plan the next scam or replenish their drug supplies. After habitually being awakened on work nights, presumably by those without recognizable employment, I was ready to break my lease and look, this time, for a rental house.

So I began to check the local newspaper, the *Mason County Democrat*, for houses to rent; and before too long, I was starting out the year 1992 in my own rental house situated on the bluff top overlooking the Illinois River, just north of Havana. The landlords, Doris and Clif, and I soon became close friends, and it was then that I learned of an interesting coincidence and why they were especially pleased to have me as a tenant just across the road from their own home on the river bluffs.

In our younger years, both Doris and I once lived in Berwyn, an older suburb near Chicago, though not at the same time, and both of us had Czech ancestors. While these facts may have gained me only a small amount of favor in their eyes, it was probably my position at the INHS that most held their interest. Their good friend the late William Starrett, who once lived down the road and often visited Clif and Doris in the 1960s, had, in 1957, initiated the fish-monitoring project I was hired to manage; he often spoke to Clif and Doris of the Illinois River and its many problems before passing away in 1972. But the fish project has been conducted most summers ever since, and I was just one of many who have carried on with the Starrett project. After I became a frequent dinner guest at Doris and Clif's home, they were again to hear firsthand accounts of the Illinois River fish project. And I, in turn, was treated to excellent food and a variety of memorable conversations, occasionally gaining an insight into what William Starrett once thought of the Illinois River and its prospects for the future.

When I arrived on the scene in Havana, my first task was to familiarize myself with as much of the previously completed Illinois River research as I could find. Next, I had to become proficient at duplicating William Starrett's method of sampling river fish, which involves using a gas-powered electric generator mounted on a john boat, with three metal rods dangling in the water off the bow. The mild voltage shocks any fish in the immediate vicinity of the boat, temporarily immobilizing them, which allows each fish to be netted from the water and placed into a large holding tank. After one hour of electrofishing, in which the boat is kept in constant motion along a predetermined route, all of the fish in the tank are identified, measured, and then returned to the river. Except for small minnows and gizzard shad, most species did not seem to be harmed by the experience. On this project, electrofishing is conducted at 26 stations along the entire Illinois River, taking just over one month to complete.

Once the fish sampling was completed each year, usually in late September, I spent most of the rest of the year managing the computerized fish database, summarizing each year's data into concise reports and presentations, and analyzing the long-term data for trends in the fish communities. The fish monitoring project, in fact, began for two main reasons: to obtain yearly information on the Illinois River's fish communities, and to indirectly assess changes in the river's ecological health by examining which species of fish were able to survive along the length of the river over time.

Today the Illinois River is still justifiably infamous as a highly degraded system, though conditions were even worse in the late 1950s before better pollution control during the following decades. Not surprisingly, better water quality has resulted in positive changes in the river's fish communities, especially on the upper Illinois River closer to Chicago. In the 1960s, for example, the common carp—a non-native species extremely tolerant of degraded waters—dominated fish catches on the electrofishing project, and less tolerant species, such as smallmouth bass, were few and far between. By the 1990s, though carp were still dominant, especially as biomass, fish diversity on the upper river had improved considerably, with several species of native sunfish and basses not at all uncommon.

Being wholly focused on this project for five years, I became very familiar with the Illinois River. But the actual field season—time spent out of the office and away from the computer—was rather short, and there was always pressure to finish the fish sampling as quickly as possible, before a freak late-summer rain might cause the river to flood, thus suspending or even canceling fish sampling. With each year, I looked less and less forward to the end of the field season and a return to the computer. And so, it was not long before I was beginning to feel the need to move on.

The INHS in Havana, though, did not have much to offer beyond what I was already doing, so moving on would mean more than switching to a different project within the INHS; it would mean leaving Havana. And this was something I did not wish to do. I felt rooted and more comfortable in my house next to Doris and Clif than at any other time in my adult life; small town life in rural central Illinois agreed with me; my circumstances of living were very much as I wished they would become when traveling through the small Mississippi River towns in northwestern Illinois and Iowa in the late 1970s. I did not want to leave behind what I had found, but professionally I was beginning to stagnate; and I never wanted to become what I had begun thinking of as a "computer biologist;" I needed something more, and with a focus that would keep me outside more often than not.

Then, just as I became resigned to sending out inquiries designed to investigate my options beyond Havana, I became aware that the Illinois Nature Preserves Commission was in the process of hiring additional field staff, with a new office being based in none other than Havana! The position would focus on securing permanent protection for high quality natural areas and managing those areas over a 22-county area, including a large portion of the Illinois River valley. Of course, I seized the opportunity and have never looked back. Since 1996, the electrofishing project has continued under the guidance of others, and it will likely continue for the foreseeable future, changing managers every few years as folks move on to other things, just as I have done. Since moving to my own home in 1999, an old farm house near Havana, I have tried to keep in touch with

Clif and Doris, but my friends have recently passed away, both living well into their 80s.

Life is quite different these days from the years when I had literally followed in the footsteps of William Starrett every September, bringing news of the river home, just as he once had done, to Clif and Doris. Such an intersection of lives can never be duplicated, and that knowledge alone has left me feeling quite privileged indeed.

Side Channels

Cattail Marsh

18

Nature Along the Margins at Cooper Park Wetlands

From the roadside of Illinois Route 116 in southwestern Woodford County, just before it plunges 250 feet down the river bluffs, one can look out onto the southwestward-oriented Illinois River valley. Like foothills from some nearby mountain range, the rounded, forested bluffs, which are ancient glacial moraines, rise abruptly from the gently meandering river valley and lower Peoria Lake. Fancy might suggest that this is a long forgotten, hidden river valley, especially if the traveler has just emerged from the rolling farmlands that cover most of central Illinois. But the river valley, of course, has a long history of human occupancy; and the results have been both positive and negative. One positive effect is called Cooper Park Wetlands, a 55-acre natural area located at the base of the river bluffs, along the margins of lower Peoria Lake.

Just before entering Tazewell County from the north, Route 116 descends the steep bluffs toward the edge of the river bottomlands; the ride is reminiscent of landing in a steady, slowly descending aircraft. The scenic view challenges the driver to remain alert. At the bottom of the bluffs, the highway soon follows along a narrow strip of land (about one quarter mile wide) between the river bluffs (rising to as much as 700 feet above sea level) and lower Peoria Lake (actually a vast widening of the Illinois River itself, which imperceptibly flows through the lake). Along this road, at the edge of East Peoria, a variety of small businesses and light industries, in strip-development fashion, are located along the highway's frontage roads. But beyond the businesses, west of Route 116, a stand of trees is barely visible. To the unknowing traveler, this stand of trees, part of Cooper Park Wetlands, may not cause much excitement, seemingly pushed by development to the edge of the lake.

While Cooper Park Wetlands is less than one-quarter mile wide, it covers nearly one mile of lakefront. A trail system runs through the entire length of the natural area as it passes through several distinctly different plant communities. The bird life is correspondingly diverse, especially during the breeding season.

The best place to begin a hike is probably at the north trailhead just south of the Spindler Marina, which, like Cooper Park Wetlands, is owned and managed by the Fon du Lac Park District. A large sign proclaims that the hiker is about to enter a "Registered Reserve." State law does, in fact, protect Cooper Park Wetlands from inappropriate development or direct destruction. A boardwalk begins after the entrance sign and leads through a wet floodplain forest dominated by silver maple, cottonwood, and green ash. From April through August, this is where the songbird chorus also begins. Warbling vireos and house wrens seemingly sound off from every direction. In spring and early summer, red-winged blackbirds and American robins are the most numerous and obvious species throughout the park. From mid-summer through September, anywhere along the trail, the laser-beam red of cardinal flower never fails to generate attention and comments.

Before too long the woods begin to open up, the ground gets wetter, and the trees shrubbier. Here the trail enters a shrub swamp dominated by black willow trees, buttonbush, and young silver maples. In areas of open marsh, inter-meshed within a mosaic of shrubs and young floodplain forest, wetland species such as arrowhead, arrow arum, and smartweed combine to create a much thicker ground cover than in the densely shaded floodplain forest, where, in places, ground cover can be rather sparse. In summer, in areas of open marsh, the large pinkish-white flowers of hibiscus, the less gaudy swamp milkweed, and the invasive non-native purple loosestrife are also very obvious. The shrub swamp is the best and most reliable place to see and hear yellow warblers, but only during the height of the breeding season; by July, they will be hard to find. In the marsh openings, one may see the occasional foraging great blue heron or the shy green heron, looking very much like a crow flying off, with a call that sounds a bit like a cat regurgitating a hairball.

The boardwalk soon passes over a series of beaver ponds, sometimes wholly covered over with a mat of floating duckweed, a small flowering aquatic plant only a few tenths of an inch in width, that many mistakenly call green algae. Where one of the beaver dams is only a few feet away, it is easy to see the water slowly trickling through the dam. Further to the east is another beaver dam, and toward the lake is another, all in perfect repair and holding back just enough water to meet design specifications. Should a breach occur, it would be quickly detected by the beavers, who will soon effect sufficient repairs. This is a good location to search for tree stumps bearing teeth marks from the perspicacious, gnawing rodents. The ponds sometimes hold resting waterfowl, most likely mallards and wood ducks, but the beavers will probably remain elusive.

Along the boardwalk is the best place to view the decurrent false aster, a federally threatened plant that has its main population distribution limited to the Illinois River valley. The decurrent false aster, which blooms in August and September, is known as a "fugitive species," which tends to rapidly colonize soil left bare from disturbances. It soon loses out in competition with other plant species, and fails to survive and reproduce after only a few years. The species is, therefore, dependent upon the formation of other newly disturbed areas for colonization.

Yearly spring floods along the Illinois River are the main mechanism that clears areas of competing vegetation, allowing colonization by the decurrent false aster. The plant has adapted over thousands of years to the river's natural hydrology, which is characterized by a gradual rise in river levels beginning in winter, a mid-spring peak flood, followed by a gradual decline to stable, low water levels throughout the summer.

The river's annual spring flood, in fact, is the critical mechanism that is essential to maintaining all of the river's natural communities of plants and animals. For many years, however, the Illinois River's watershed has been highly modified by levee-building, ditching, drain tiles, urbanization, intensive row-cropping, and stream channelization. The result has been that for many decades water has been delivered to the main stem river at a much more rapid rate than before intensive agriculture. This allows for more frequent floods, even during the summer growing season, when the plants are "expecting" stable, low water levels. Water level changes also occur as a response to operation of the lock and dam system. And the river's water is now seemingly perpetually turbid due to its high-suspended sediment load from erosion across the watershed. Plants that are adapted to surviving under water for brief periods may now, thus, be enshrouded in darkness until the water recedes. It is little wonder, then, that a plant such as the decurrent false aster is threatened with extinction. The large Peoria lakes (lower and upper), in any case, tend to buffer water level changes during the growing season; and perhaps that is why the decurrent false aster persists at Cooper Park Wetlands.

From shrub swamp and open marsh, the Cooper Park trail leaves the boardwalk to enter a more mature stand of floodplain forest. This is one of the better places to see a prothonotary warbler—in season, of course. If there is one songbird that can be called a floodplain forest specialty, it is the cavity-nesting prothonotary warbler. The prothonotary warbler even seems to have an affinity for nesting in forests with standing water around the nest tree. Unable to create its own nest hole, the prothonotary warbler may use an old woodpecker hole excavated in a standing dead tree.

The trail continues through the forest and eventually leaves one of the two Registered Reserve units. To the east is a manicured picnic area; to the west is lower Peoria Lake. Before continuing on the trail, it is worthwhile to walk to the lake's sandy shoreline to look for terns, gulls, double-crested cormorants, and waterfowl. Because the Illinois River valley is a major migratory flyway, a birder should be prepared for anything.

In recent years, American white pelicans have been using the river valley during migration; they may typically be seen leisurely soaring in great slow-moving flocks high over head or seriously following one another, first up a short way, and then down over invisible air waves, tracing sine waves across the sky. During appropriate times of the spring and fall migratory periods, seeing a low-flying osprey can almost be counted upon. Bald eagles are an absolute certainty during the winter months. Without mud flats in the immediate area, large numbers of shorebirds can be ruled out; but killdeer should be expected, and spotted sandpipers can sometimes be seen bobbing their tails along the margins of the lake or across fallen logs. From July through September, astronomical numbers of swallows may be seen flying in every direction, from just above the water to hundreds of feet in the air. With only a small degree of persistence, one may see cliff, barn, bank, northern rough-winged, and tree swallows, plus purple martins.

At lower Peoria Lake's shoreline, the shining, tall buildings of downtown Peoria are clearly visible two miles away, as are the upscale condominiums and strip developments just outside the boundaries of Cooper

Park. The gambling boat and hotel complex further down the shore add the Las Vegas touch. It is this view that underscores the significance of the sliver of undeveloped, wild land that is Cooper Park Wetlands.

The south unit of Cooper Park Wetlands Reserve begins at an area that was only very recently kept mowed and manicured. Now, however, the natural process of plant succession is being left to its own devices here, where young cottonwood and silver maple saplings, plus a few other species, are competing for dominance. This area will continue to change in structure and plant composition as the winners at competition for space, water, nutrients, and sunlight become the dominant individuals. Here, decurrent false aster once grew, but that stage, just after the mowing stopped, has long passed. Decurrent false aster is now elsewhere. Trees grow fast on the floodplain, though, so it will not be long before this thicket of saplings resembles more mature forests. Thicket-loving bird species such as the common yellowthroat, brown thrasher, and gray catbird will find appropriate habitats here for a few years—until the trees mature, when they will be forced to seek shrublands elsewhere. Change, of course, is the nature of succession.

The Cooper Park trail continues southward past the early successional woods into a more mature floodplain forest. Here, as in other areas of the forest, one may take notice of piles of woody debris covering the forest floor in many places. Much of this wood has continually been piled and re-distributed by floodwaters. It is not unusual for the entire trail system, including the boardwalk, to be covered in water during peak flood times during the spring. Park management policy includes leaving the woody debris piles in place because of the wildlife values such structures provide.

Before leaving the reserve's southern entrance, the trail passes over another boardwalk system, which gives access to additional willow-shrub wetlands and forest. Bird communities here are similar to those already encountered, although subtle differences, due to varying habitat characteristics, become evident upon closer inspection.

A traveler on Illinois Route 116 intent upon the larger, more well-known natural attractions of Illinois might be more focused on getting as far away from gambling boats and pseudo-Floridian strip developments as quickly as possible. The stand of trees at Cooper Park Wetlands between the strip of businesses and the margins of lower Peoria Lake would quickly pass behind un-noticed. Cooper Park Wetlands, though, provides a good excuse to slow down, pull off the highway, and take a lazy hike for an hour or so. There are few better ways for adding balance to your life.

Side Channels

19

As the Rivers Rise Again

Yesterday was the 2008 Summer Solstice. Today the sun is hot once again, and the afternoon winds rapidly desiccate the sandy soils of Mason County, Illinois, stressing our growing vegetable garden. So my wife and I hope for more rain, despite the fact that this spring has been particularly cool and rainy. Those abundant rains over the last few weeks have produced a spectacular wildflower display in my reconstructed sand prairie and encouraged a healthy spring growth in my ten-year-old oak and hickory trees. But, unfortunately, those same rains have resulted in widespread flooding across the Midwest—flooding on a scale that has been compared only with the Great Flood of 1993 on the Mississippi River.

In 1993, I was also living high and dry as events slowly and daily unfolded around me. Safe as I was, it was difficult to discern the true magnitude and scale of the flooding of the Mississippi and its tributaries, as it was occurring from day to day. But after a while I began to notice that headlines with the word "flooding" were not going away; and the afternoon rains were so regular, one could almost tell the time of day by the mid-afternoon peal of thunder and lightning that seemed to appear from nowhere even on the sunniest of days.

Then the big rivers began cresting and the levees breaking. Small river towns that few had ever heard of were suddenly in the media spotlight. Obscure places such as Grafton, Illinois and St. Genevieve, Missouri became synonymous with disaster or impending disaster. And today, the same place names are rolling off the media tongue once again; until, like the last time, the floodwaters recede, and folks are left to deal with the aftermath and to wait until the next big flood.

Many of those who were flooded out in 1993 have moved off of the floodplains, but many have stayed, and new developments on the floodplains have continued. Even though everyone knows the rivers will flood again, when and how high can never be predicted with any comfortable degree of certainty. The 1993 flood has been called a 500-year flood. Gamblers understand such terminology. There is a 1-in-500 chance of a flood as large as the 1993 flood occurring in any given year. But a similar event could still occur next year or not for 1000 years or more. What is certain, though, is that once a 500-year flood occurs, it is absolutely wrong to expect that a comparable flood will definitely not occur for another 500 years. Misinterpretation of this statistic continues, sometimes with fatal consequences.

On this hot June day it is, of course, impossible to know how events will play out this time. The massive rainstorms of earlier in the month seem to have passed. But will they return next week? The week after? As anyone with even minimal experience with rivers knows, the spring flood is a normal part of a river's yearly cycle in the Midwest, just as summer droughts are also part of the cycle, when the rivers fall to their lowest levels. But will they fall to normal this time before going back up again next spring? Or will 2008 harbor a worse disaster than 1993?

As distant thunder peals outside of my office window this afternoon, the sun continues to shine. And except for the isolated storm to the west, the skies look as peaceful and inviting as a summer day could be. And so it was in 1993.

[Author's Note: The summer of 2008 did, indeed, see record flooding in some areas of the Mississippi River, but not on the scale of the 1993 event.]

Side Channels

20
The Gizzard Shad in Nature's Economy

One freezing winter day while walking along the Illinois River near Havana, I noticed thousands of fish swimming in the clear water near shore. Most of them were gizzard shad, small-to-medium-sized members of the herring family. Gizzard shad tend to be rather numerous throughout the river, forming an important food source for populations of many bird species, especially overwintering bald eagles.

The shad I saw in the shallow water that day, in fact, were easy prey, especially those that were showing signs of stress from the recent period of prolonged frigid temperatures. Common goldeneyes, mergansers, and gulls had a feast on the dead shad floating in the open water. And soon I saw a bald eagle leave its perch on an upper branch of a tall cottonwood tree to fly over the expanse of frozen river. The eagle decreased its altitude in a series of graceful turns, then extended its talons forward just as it was barely above a patch of open water; it grabbed a fish from the water, and then flew to a silver maple tree to feed. Of no surprise to me, the fish in the eagle's talons was a gizzard shad.

From those simple observations, it was easy to see the relationships between gizzard shad and the fish-eating birds. But it made me wonder about the shad themselves. What do they feed on? And what aspects of life history and behavior explain their importance to other river inhabitants?

Obtaining Food

Water in the Illinois River teams with a variety of microscopic life called "plankton," which is derived from the Greek word *planktos*, meaning "drifting" or "wandering." The animals of the plankton are called "zooplankton," the plants "phytoplankton." There are a bewildering variety of types and sizes of these plankters, from one-celled protozoans, invisible to the unaided eye, to minute crustaceans that one can just barely see darting about below the water's surface. These are small animals, indeed, with perhaps many thousand per cubic meter of water, depending on river conditions and time of year. The phytoplankton are generally even smaller than the zooplankton, and even more numerous. But these small organisms, drifting about in the river's sluggish currents, are a major component of a gizzard shad's diet, although the proportion of zooplankton or phytoplankton in the diet changes with the age of the fish.

Below a length of about one inch, a young shad looks and behaves like a carnivore. Its mouth is lined with small teeth and is farther forward on the body than in the adult fish; these features facilitate the capture of live prey. The digestive tract of shad at this stage is short, a reflection of the easier digestibility of animal versus vegetable matter. At this immature life stage, the shad compete with the young of other fish species for the same prey, which is mainly zooplankton. Most fish species switch to other prey as they grow older. Young shad travel about in schools to increase foraging efficiency and to protect themselves from larger predators, such as largemouth bass. They form schools to confuse predators with a complicated motion—much as birds in a flock.

When a young shad grows to about one inch in length, its body goes through a major transformation, and its diet gradually begins to include more plant material. The digestive tract becomes long and twisted, a necessity due to the longer time required to digest plants. In addition, the teeth are lost, and the mouth gradually moves slightly toward the bottom side of the fish, reflecting its new non-predatory lifestyle. Adult gizzard shad feed heavily on phytoplankton in addition to a variety of dead, decaying animal and plant matter collectively called "detritus." They also ingest mud and attached algae, which are simple plants that grow on solid objects in water clear enough to allow sunlight to filter through. Adult shad are, therefore, plant eaters, or herbivores, as well as detritivores.

Adult shad forage by filter-feeding, as opposed to actively pursuing zooplankters as they did when young. They do not, however, passively filter the water while moving slowly forward with their mouths agape as one might imagine; instead, they actively pump-filter the water by drawing a definite volume into the mouth cavity. Food particles and minute organisms are then strained from the water by special structures called "gill rakers" at the back of the mouth cavity.

Because each food particle filtered from the water contains only a small amount of energy, large volumes of water must be pumped into the mouth and filtered for food items. The ability to acquire energy from such diffuse resources as phytoplankton and detritus hints at the important role played by adult gizzard shad in the riverine environment.

Energy Flow Through the Ecosystem

For ecosystems (a term that refers to the community of all living organisms more or less within a definite area, plus their habitats), sunlight is the driving energy force; and, needless to say, without sunlight, an ecosystem would eventually run down. Plants are the primary producers; they are able to combine carbon dioxide with sunlight and water through photosynthesis to form sugar, a form of stored energy. The plants, whether eaten directly by herbivores or as dead plant material in detritus, form the base of the ecosystem's food chains. Mid-level carnivores (for example, ten-day-old shad) may feed on zooplankters that in turn had fed on plants. Top carnivores, in the strictest sense, do not feed on plants; but if we look at the food of their prey and so on, eventually we will come to plants. So a largemouth bass could have fed on a warmouth sunfish, which had fed on an aquatic insect that in turn had grazed on plant materials; but the warmouth may also have fed on a crayfish that ate mostly plant detritus, or may even have scavenged on a dead bluegill. Where does the gizzard shad fit into this picture? We have seen that it holds many roles in the riverine ecosystem, beginning life midway up the food chain as a carnivore, and then settling down in adulthood closer to the bottom. Food chains, in fact, are so interwoven that all of the food chains in an ecosystem can be referred to as a food web.

As energy moves up a food web, from the sun to plants to top carnivores, most of it is lost due to the inefficiency of transfer from one level to another. Because of the inevitable energy losses with each level up a food web, the closer an animal can feed to the base of the web (the plants), the more energy will be available. This is where the gizzard shad plays a significant role. To be sure, there are many other fish species in the river, but the non-native silver carp is the only other species feeding at the base of the food web that is so abundant, widespread, and easily available as a food resource for carnivores. The rapid growth of shad (to about four inches in length after the first growing season) ensures a minimum of delay and energy loss in transferring energy from the sun through the shad's plant foods into animal life that can be utilized by such large carnivores as the bald eagle.

Producing the Next Generation

The gizzard shad belongs to a general category of organisms of diverse kinds whose life history strategies include high reproductive potential with little or no parental care of the young. At the other extreme are organisms that invest much time, care, and resources into raising only a few young. Birds belong to this second category, an extreme example of which is the California condor that lays only one egg, and may not breed every year. Between these two extremes are many variations. Sunfish, for instance, lay many eggs, but actually construct nests and protect the eggs and newly hatched young from predators.

Gizzard shad in the Illinois River probably spawn in backwater areas, sloughs, or quiet coves beginning in April or May, when rising water temperatures are between 50 and 70° F, and they may continue through June. A spring flood in the river is beneficial to the shad because the greater volume of water increases the available spawning and rearing habitat. When spawning, females release thousands of eggs into the water column. The eggs, each about three quarters of a millimeter in diameter, are fertilized by the males, then sink and become attached to any solid object. They hatch about four days later. About five days after hatching, the young shad begin actively feeding.

The high reproductive output of the gizzard shad is one reason why the population can endure winter die-offs and heavy predation. Even so, their populations tend to vary considerably from one year to another.

A Web of Interactions

The changes in shad populations from year to year must surely have effects on other riverine life. For instance, more shad might mean more food for bass, allowing for greater survival of bass to larger sizes and possibly better reproduction from healthier individuals; then, more and larger bass might result in greater predation on other fish species, including shad. More shad would also result in greater predation on plankton. One might imagine many other similar scenarios.

Side Channels

In 1869, John Muir wrote that, "When we try to pick out anything by itself, we find it hitched to everything in the universe." It is a concept worth thinking about when watching a bald eagle forage for gizzard shad or, at a much greater scale, when viewing the night sky full of stars; the concept might even make it easier to appreciate life in the depths of the murky Illinois River or a community of aquatic plants and animals invisible to the naked eye. It might even help us understand where we humans fit into the big picture, within the world's great food web. Such an ecological perspective is necessary today more than ever, as the human population continues to grow and prosper, demanding increasingly greater amounts of the earth's natural resources.

Watching the Mississippi River at Bear Creek, Illinois

Side Channels

21

In Praise of Sitting and Staring

Early in the 1970s I first heard Bob Dylan's song "Watching the River Flow," and, probably because I had already developed a growing fascination for rivers, it grabbed my attention. Since that time, not only have I not grown tired of the song, but, interestingly, it has followed me through life—a life during which I have collectively spent many hours watching numerous rivers flow, learning the gentle art of quietly sitting and observing.

In our society, though, with its worthy emphasis on making tangible accomplishments, such idleness is frowned upon. Indeed, I suspect that most would feel guilty to simply lean against a riverbank tree, taking in the surroundings; not fishing, not hunting, not gathering morel mushrooms; just listening and watching. Admit to engaging in this activity more than once, and one may likely be labeled a "good for nothing." A fair enough assessment, I must admit, on the surface.

But where the body may be idle, the mind and soul are not. A heightened awareness results from remaining still, actually quite an active mental state that is not preoccupied with physical activity. I recall many experiences immediately after reclining against a steep riverbank, first beginning to notice each bird and insect sound from near and far; then the very slight movements of plants in the merest shifts of air—not even enough to be called a breeze; changes in temperature from one side of my face to the other, one in the sun, the other shaded; sunlight filtering through layers of leaves—flecks of light throughout the forest continually changing shape as the sun moves and cloud patterns shift; a river's flow discernable by countless minute bits of debris carried along with the current, occasionally a small twig or large log, maybe even an entire tree; boils on the water's surface where the current is forced upward from a large, submerged object; circular eddies where moving water is drawn downward; a musty scent of humidity and rotting organic matter carried on a momentary breeze. Nothing is ever the same from one moment to the next. No reruns.

The mind freewheels and wanders to the past, speculates on the future, contemplates the passing moments. New ideas emerge from the depths. Until some outstanding sight or sound breaks my concentration, and I might look to where the river curves around a bend, curious as to what may be there and realizing I do not know the time of day or how long I have been lost to my senses. So by instinct, I may determine that it is time to move on, eventually to face the pressing issues of the day and responsibilities that I have become expert at putting off.

So what have I accomplished by this sitting and staring, at those moments when I have sat to watch a river flow, when I hear that Dylan song in my mind? Perhaps nothing. Unless it may be considered an accomplishment to have slowed down my life but momentarily. For a middle-aged life that seems to be passing more quickly with each year, that is quite satisfying.

Part Two
Travel

Trempealeau Mountain, Upper Mississippi River, Wisconsin

Side Channels

22

Pursuing the Blue Goose Across Illinois

In contrast to states like North Dakota or Alaska, Illinois' National Wildlife Refuges seem to exhibit a relatively low profile, not being dominant features of the overall landscape, performing their functions quite well without much fanfare. So, as a personal tribute to the National Wildlife Refuge System's 2003 Centennial, I embarked upon a journey in late April 2003 to visit Illinois' 11 National Wildlife Refuges (NWR) within a two-week period. I logged about 1,900 miles, traveled from the far southern tip of the state to the far northwestern corner, and experienced quite a few moments of inspiration and a few of tribulation. And I kept a journal.

Crab Orchard Refuge

Before too long, there were two ticks on my pants!
–April 22, 2003, journal

Side Channels

    My initial encounter with the Crab Orchard Refuge on this trip was at its visitor contact station along Illinois Route 148. This 44,000-acre upland refuge straddles Illinois' Southern Till Plain and Shawnee Hills. At the station, I learned of the area's complex history, remnants of which still exist. For example, by congressional mandate, Crab Orchard Refuge supports an industrial park, which employs hundreds in many of the same buildings that were once used to manufacture military ordnance during World War II. Farming still occurs on about 5,000 acres of refuge land. To avoid conflicts of use and for reasons of safety (especially from known areas with hazardous wastes), about half of the refuge is closed to public access.

    While I cannot say that I felt unwelcome surrounded by closed areas, I soon retreated from the busy contact station to Devil's Kitchen Lake, one of three large reservoirs on the refuge fully open to the public and adjacent to Crab Orchard Wilderness Area. In years past, I have had some of my best wilderness canoeing experiences on Devil's Kitchen Lake. This trip proved no exception.

    Being late April, the extensive forests at Crab Orchard Refuge were loaded with migrating songbirds. Kentucky and northern parula warblers were especially numerous. In the clear skies above the lake, black vultures soared in the 20-mile-per-hour winds. There were no sounds from nearby civilization. I paddled against unpredictably strong wind gusts, dodged submerged snags, and made plans to soon finish up with the Southern Illinois refuges, before heading northward.

Cypress Creek Refuge: Gateway to the Delta

    ...not at all like entering a place (e.g., Yosemite National Park) and knowing you are 'inside.'
–April 23, 2003, journal

Cypress Creek Refuge follows along the Cache River through the bottomlands of Southern Illinois' Coastal Plain, the northernmost reaches of the Lower Mississippi River Delta and the South. The power of the big rivers in this region of Illinois cannot be overstated, as thousands of years ago the Ohio River once flowed through parts of the Cache River valley before abruptly changing its course during a massive flood event. And during the Great Flood of 1993, after the rivers had supposedly long been under our control, the Mississippi River nearly changed its course in far southern Alexander County. This would have shortened the river by about 13 miles. On this trip I would see other effects of the 1993 flood many times at other refuges.

Cypress Creek Refuge may still best be described as a work-in-progress. I never really did find the refuge headquarters, and my impression was that much of the area within the 35,000-acre acquisition boundary is still a mosaic of public and private lands. Border signs bearing the familiar "Blue Goose" of the National Wildlife Refuge lands were here and there, but more often than not, it was difficult to determine whether a piece of land was private or public. With little time for exploration, I drove southward, attempting to stay as close to the Cache River as possible. With few areas to access the lower Cache River, I contented myself with spying the occasional Blue Goose sign from the highway to remind myself that Cypress Creek Refuge was not far away.

My visit to Illinois' refuges had now turned into a river trip. I would follow the Mississippi River northward and then the Illinois River. And what better place to start than at the confluence of the Mississippi and Ohio rivers at Fort Defiance Park? Here I sat for a few minutes on the piles of rock used to stabilize the riverbank; on the right was the Mississippi, on the left the Ohio. At over one mile in width below the confluence, the Mississippi stood alone, second to no other river in North America, waters from New York to Montana mingling in one massive, muddy, rolling, and eddying force of nature.

Mississippi River Refuges

The character of the water drew my attention...I imagined the river draining the North Woods.
–April 28, 2003, journal

Following the Great River Road northward from Cairo and past Fountain Bluff, I soon began looking for Blue Goose signs along a levee road, which marks the eastern boundary of the 2,770-acre Wilkinson Island Division of the Middle Mississippi River Refuge. This refuge is part of the Mark Twain National Wildlife Refuge Complex (which also includes Two Rivers NWR, Great River NWR, and Port Louisa NWR), a scattering of refuge lands along the Mississippi River reaching as far north as Muscatine, Iowa.

The levee road descends about 20 feet to the bottomlands, and then follows a muddy access road into the interior. Much of the forests on both sides of the road were stands of young pole-sized (about 6 inches in diameter) willows, cottonwoods, and silver maples. I imagined they began growth shortly after the recession of the 1993 floodwaters, a truly fantastic benchmark in time.

Further along the trail, near an old levee break, I came upon a great bowl-sized depression (perhaps 100 feet in diameter) filled with water. It looked like a manmade pond, but actually it was a scour hole, where the levee had been breached during the 1993 flood. The water looked shallow, but probably was scoured to as much as 50 feet deep when the floodwaters breached the levee in a torrential waterfall of power, debris, and destruction. The river asserted its hegemony; and, after the government appropriated funds to purchase flood-prone lands, the Middle Mississippi River Refuge was born.

Along the Great River Road, heading westward from Alton, Illinois, the Mississippi is more like a lake than ever. The Melvin Price Lock and Dam (#26) has raised the water level and slowed the current of the natural river, which is especially noticeable during the summer low-water period. On this day in late April, however, the river was inching up toward its regular spring flood, and was acting like a river again...almost. The wind blew about 30 miles per hour from the east in opposition to the river's current flow, which, in this stretch of the river, is toward the east. Massive swells and white caps resulted, similar to what one might find on the Great Lakes. Had I been foolish enough to launch my canoe, it would have been swamped in a minute. So I gave up plans to visit the Portage Island Division (230 acres) of Two Rivers Refuge, and simply pulled to the side of the road to search trees along the island (about one mile distant) for Blue Goose signs.

The Gilbert Lake Division (736 acres) of Two Rivers Refuge is actually along the Illinois River, just upstream from the confluence of the Illinois and Mississippi rivers. I would return to the Illinois River at a later date, but at that point in time, I thought it best to take advantage of the break in storm activity by hiking the Gilbert Lake Trail, which follows along a natural levee parallel to the river. Woods along the Illinois River provided foraging habitat for many migrating songbirds. Soon a prothonotary warbler sang, and over the river, with a little persistence, I saw all six species of Illinois' swallows. In a willow thicket, I heard the first yellow warbler of the year. Red-tailed hawks soared on updrafts over the river bluffs, but on this hike the trees made the greatest impression. Few places along the Illinois River have such healthy stands of pecan trees. These mast-producing trees in the hickory family form a very valuable component of floodplain forests by producing a yearly nut crop. At the Gilbert

Lake Division, they are massive and tall, with huge spreading canopies. Sapling pecans, though, are few, which ultimately does not bode well for future stands.

After a quick stop at the Two Rivers Refuge headquarters on the Calhoun Division (4,835 acres), I headed back to the Mississippi River at the Batchtown Division (3,500 acres). While dangerous storm clouds gathered, birds were scarce. Even over the Mississippi, there was little activity. They knew better than I, of course, that no intelligent creature would remain vulnerable with such weather on the way. I barely made it back to my vehicle before the clouds burst. And had I driven the slightly muddy road to the river instead of walking, my soccer-mom mini-van would have been hopelessly mired.

Following a day layover, I was back on the road again bound for the Great River Refuge. After searching quite a while for signs bearing the Blue Goose, I finally found the entrance to the Delair Division (1,715 acres) across from Louisiana, Missouri. But, for whatever reason, most of this refuge is closed to public access. I glanced at the Mississippi River and a few great egrets foraging in the shallows, then quickly headed north to the Great River Refuge's Long Island Division (6,300 acres), just upstream of Quincy, Illinois.

The river was running fast on the day of my visit, building toward its spring crest right on schedule; it would be a cakewalk float downstream in a canoe, but a real fight getting back. The side channels were filled with powerboats, and the woods teamed with morel mushroom hunters. Because conditions narrowly favored hiking over canoeing, I looked for and found a large tree under which to sit, read, and think about the eight-mile-long Long Island, just visible downstream and across the side channel from my vantage point.

Several years ago, during late summer, I had set out to explore Long Island. The plan had been to canoe into the island's interior via one of several shallow, long, and narrow sloughs. These would lead me to the old-growth forests, which were my objective.

The entrance to one of the sloughs marked the first of several difficulties: a small sandbar blocked its entrance. So I was forced to drag the canoe and its contents over the sandbar to deeper water, which was actually just barely deep enough for my heavily laden canoe. Of course, the slough soon became shallower. So I hid all of my gear in some brush, chained the canoe to a tree, and tried to remember not to lose the key.

Soon a massive bur oak tree came into view. Later there were several more, with pin oak, shellbark hickory, pecan, and sycamore; these were species of the original bottomland forests (regenerating bottomland forests of today have a higher component of flood-tolerant silver maple and green ash, less oak and hickory). Their sizes told the story. I had found the old growth! But the woods had been severely damaged from prolonged flooding in 1993. Much of the forest floor was a tangle of woody debris fallen from dead or dying trees, and all was covered in vines. Walking was difficult at best. There is comfort, though, in knowing that these forests are safe from logging, and the forests will eventually recover.

Following the aborted visit to Long Island on this Blue Goose trip, I next followed a direct route to extreme northwestern Illinois and the Upper Mississippi River National Wildlife and Fish Refuge, a roughly 200,000-acre refuge that stretches 260 miles from Illinois to Minnesota. At the Savanna District headquarters in Thomson, Illinois, maps were available showing the fine details of Mississippi River pools 12 to 14 (the length of the refuge in Illinois). I scanned for birds in the refuge's Clinton Lake and Spring Lake, and was placing my canoe into the river at Blanding Landing (about 10 miles south of Galena) by 5:30 p.m.

Early evening on the river was windless, cool, and clear. Majestic bluffs of the Driftless Area, untouched by Pleistocene Ice Age glaciers, flanked the river on both sides, rising like mountains, with their trees just beginning to leaf out this far north—an idyllic setting. The river ran swiftly, even close to shore, but paddling upstream required only a slight effort.

After a while, I beached my canoe on an island, with floodwaters nearly even with its surface, and settled in for a picnic dinner and reading. Wood ducks crossed my view now and then, and a muskrat swam across the channel several times. And I recalled a quarter century before, the first time I had seen the Upper Mississippi River Refuge, from the cliffs of Mississippi Palisades State Park, not very far from where I sat that evening. I, a punk, had ridden a motorcycle from Chicago, arriving at the cliff edge just as a turkey vulture took flight. The river valley seemed to be an untouched, trackless wilderness; and I longed to walk within its forests and canoe its waters.

Today I am under no illusions. The river may have its wilderness moments, but with its lock and dam system, rip-rap-stabilized banks in many areas, wing dams extending perpendicularly from its banks, levees constricting its lateral movement, and dredged navigation channel, the Mississippi River has become a highly altered and manipulated system. The National Wildlife Refuges, in fact, are the upper river's outstanding natural features. And it would please me a great deal to say the same after the next 25 years.

After returning to my vehicle and loading the canoe, my thoughts were still wistfully lost in the past, as my driving skills must also have been; for when I heard a loud boom and crash as I was backing out of my parking space, I was jolted back to the present and the reality of a totally shattered rear window caused from backing my van into the corner of a large garbage bin. In a microsecond, there went my idyllic evening and my tax refund! I would finish this refuge journey with the help of a plastic bag and duct tape.

The 1,400-acre Keithsburg Division of the Port Louisa Refuge was the last of the Mississippi River refuges on my list. For a short period, I watched a spotted sandpiper foraging along a floating log, and tree swallows aerially defending territories around numerous snags (more remnants of the 1993 flood). Leaving my gear-filled vehicle unattended with its smashed window was out of the question. So with only the Illinois River refuges left to visit on this trip, I vowed to return later in the year to canoe the complex of backwater lakes and channels that beckoned in the distance.

Illinois River Refuges

...siltation is a problem...but the shallow conditions tend to keep power boaters away; there is something positive in nearly everything....
−April 26, 2003, journal

Four refuges comprise The Illinois River National Wildlife and Fish Refuges: Cameron-Billsbach Unit, Chautauqua Refuge, Emiquon Refuge, and Meredosia Refuge. Meredosia Refuge (3,300 acres), along the lower Illinois River, was first on my list. Lake Meredosia is the refuge's main feature. Not all of the lake, however, is federally owned. Blue Goose signs are posted along the access road and on the far shore in several places, but on the water it was still difficult to determine exactly where the refuge began or ended. In contrast to my unwillingness to trespass, a flock of American white pelicans, numerous pairs of wood ducks, hundreds of tree swallows, and red-winged blackbirds failed to acknowledge the official refuge boundaries. So I followed their lead and settled in for the evening, my canoe slowly drifting in no particular direction in the light breezes. The wildlife and I had the refuge to ourselves, a common circumstance, in fact.

At Emiquon Refuge (2,114 acres), I parked in a small lot just north of where the Spoon River flows beneath the Illinois Route 97/78 bridge, and then hiked the north bank of the Spoon River to its confluence with the Illinois, just opposite Havana. The Emiquon Refuge is much more than a work-in-progress, but when federal acquisitions are someday complete, Blue Goose signs will border 11,122 acres.

Floodplain forests and backwater sloughs dominate areas along the Spoon River. Other portions of the Emiquon Refuge include flood-prone areas recovering from agriculture or soon to be retired from crops. I followed the bank of the Illinois River upstream to a large levee, the refuge's current boundary. A great blue heron flew past nearly at eye level, bound, no doubt, for one of the nearby rookeries. From my vantage point on top of the levee, I could barely discern a line of trees, about three miles upstream, that marked Chautauqua Refuge's southern boundary.

Chautauqua Refuge (4,488 acres) offers a different way to experience the Illinois River valley: a visitor may follow a gravel road along the top of a levee system which divides Lake Chautauqua into two pools and separates both from the Illinois River. One evening, I followed the south levee, riding a bicycle on what I consider to be one of the finest bike routes in the state, although the gravel-topped levee is a bit rough. The levee road passes through floodplain forests, upland sand forests, lakes, wetlands, and backwater sloughs. At Eagle Bluff Access, an active bald eagle nest is actually quite visible within a stand of dead timber. The eight-mile bike trip is one I often repeat.

The final refuge on this tour was the obscure Cameron-Billsbach Unit (1,709 acres). Probably the best way to access this refuge unit is from the Illinois River. So with my canoe once again strapped to the top of my vehicle, I headed for Marshall County. Just south of Henry, I noticed two Blue Goose signs east of the highway, apparently the only access to the Cameron- Billsbach Unit from land (without trespassing, that is). I parked on a dirt lane and hiked to the nearby bottomlands, soon encountering a fairly extensive beaver dam, a foraging solitary sandpiper on the dam, and a female hooded merganser on the water. It was a great wildlife viewing spot, but the Illinois River was waiting.

The wind helped carry my canoe downstream from Henry's boat ramp. Warblers sang from the floodplain forests, which were quickly retreating rearward. Several Forster's terns leisurely followed the river northward, occasionally diving into the river to catch fish. At Upper Henry Island and Billsbach Lake there were ring-billed gulls and more terns. Here I began searching for Blue Goose signs, and actually found more than one attached to fallen trees, destined to be carried away by the next flood. Nesting Canada geese sounded alarm calls as I hiked the length of the refuge's Upper Henry Island. Then not until I completely paddled out of the area back toward Henry did they become quiet once more.

After visiting the Cameron-Billsbach Unit, my goal of visiting all of Illinois' National Wildlife Refuges within a two-week period had been realized. And what better recommendation can I give to the U.S. Fish and Wildlife Service than this: "I shall return." Of course, the river will continue to flood as it normally does and occasionally in a catastrophic way, influencing the refuges as it does so, challenging the refuge managers. But I am confident that they are up to the challenge.

Side Channels

23

Eulogy for an Oak

Edwin Way Teale once wrote about revisiting a favorite wild place after a long absence:

> *On a return to old familiar scenes, it is remarkable how remembered trees seem to step forward to meet you in a landscape...they are landmarks of special importance. We look over the old trees as we do our dear friends and acquaintances to note the changes that the years have brought.*

Similar thoughts were passing through my mind as I neared a longtime favorite forest preserve near Chicago following several years of absence. For quite a few years beginning in the mid-1980s and before moving to Southern Illinois, I had been a regular, almost weekly, visitor to the natural areas near Spear Woods. During this time, I had established a fairly regular route through the woods and fields, mostly following animal trails. Many of my hikes began just after sunrise when few other humans were about. A large white oak tree marked the furthest point on most hikes; after sitting for a while against the oak, I would usually begin to head back to the trail head on 95th street. As I left my vehicle in the preserve parking area on this return October visit, I could clearly envision the old oak. Little did I know that a big change had occurred during my extended absence.

An Outdoor Education

Like most previous hikes, I followed a frequently used deer trail on the way to my favorite white oak tree, passing near Pollywog Slough. Because of the frequency of my former visits to the Spear Woods area, I had become extremely familiar with the lay of the land, the different bird species to be found at all seasons, and the timing of their migrations. After a while, I even became familiar with individual plants along the trails. At the northernmost point of Pollywog Slough is a stand of prairie cordgrass, which, probably because of its rarity in the area and its association with wild, uncultivated land, has always seemed to provide me with a vague sense of security for the future of the natural world; how long it has been there will never be certain.

Walking past the slough, I remembered that prior to the drought of 1988, the slough was mostly open water. Since the drought, it has become overgrown with plants, mostly cattails. The drought seems to have pushed ahead the natural plant succession, tending toward a forest. On a previous trip, when there was still much open water at the slough, I had watched the complicated flights of numerous barn and rough-winged swallows picking insects from the air and off the water's surface. I recalled how the late afternoon sunlight reflected from the barn swallows' feathers, making the tops of their bodies a deep blue, richer in quality than the early evening sky of a clear Canadian high.

Hogwash Slough was my next stopping place on the trail toward the old oak tree, and a rotting log covered with mosses provided a good vantage point to watch for birds over the water. One spring there was a yellow-crowned night heron perching on the top of a dead tree, perhaps on its way to the heronries of the Lake Calumet wetlands. And once, during the fall hawk migration, I watched an osprey flying from the north; the bird circled over the slough a few times, and then dove into the water, emerging a few seconds later with a small fish in its talons. The osprey then perched on the top of a dead tree and fed on the fish for several minutes before continuing southward. I remembered summer months with red-headed woodpeckers and cedar waxwings flying back and forth over the slough catching insects from the air, while from time to time a belted kingfisher hovered over the water, its body seemingly anchored to a point in the air. Though I had been using this same log for years, a large clump of the non-native multiflora rose now grew in front of the log, obscuring my view of the slough. On future hikes I would have to find a new log.

North of Hogwash Slough, I followed the deer trail to an old field containing a great deal of scrubby vegetation in addition to several good-quality prairie plants: wild false indigo, wild quinine, prairie dock, and stands of big bluestem grass. It was at the meadow years ago that I first saw the old oak tree after topping a slight rise in the land. In my mind's eye, I could see its wide, open crown and large lower branches, indicating that as long as this tree was alive, the surrounding area was open with few other trees. A tree that grew to maturity in a closed-canopy forest would have had its lower branches fall away through a process of "self-pruning."

Early on I had begun to use the tree as a good place to sit, listen to the wind and birds, read, and sleep. I returned often, once to find a large bird fly from the ground on my approach in order to land on the tree's lowest branch. Slowly, the bird turned its head, and I found myself face to face with a great horned owl; its eyes seemed to indicate boredom at my presence rather than alarm. I half expected the owl to rush at me with extended talons, against which I would have been defenseless; instead, it quickly disappeared into the forest without a sound.

Most days at the tree had been somewhat less eventful. Summer days in the shade were filled with soothingly warm breezes accompanied by the continuous songs of common yellowthroats and goldfinches, occasionally a blue-winged warbler. During the winter I sometimes sighted a northern shrike or American kestrel. And in all seasons the skies usually contained soaring red-tailed hawks, some of which engaged in courtship displays beginning in late winter.

Sometimes there were mats of grass near the tree flattened from white-tailed deer resting in the night. Signs of deer are very common, from frequently encountered piles of their droppings to scattered bones. The deer, in fact, are highly overpopulated in the Cook County forest preserves. With few natural predators to check their numbers, a population boom and bust cycle may be inevitable.

As I walked toward the old oak tree on this most recent visit, I remembered these and many more experiences, and the promise of a new adventure caused me to walk a bit faster than usual. Would I see an owl on this day? A northern shrike? Or maybe a coyote, known to have increasing populations in Illinois? The answers were just over the next rise, beyond a line of oaks.

Winds of Change

Sandhill cranes in a vee-formation called from above as I came near to the field with the old oak tree. Then another, larger flock came into view, stealing my attention for several minutes. Despite the anticipation, I delayed my walk to the tree in order to watch the cranes, reasoning that the tree would still be there, while the cranes would soon be gone. But when I topped the rise in land, I was greeted with a scene not matching my memory: the old tree had fallen. Unsuspected by me, its main trunk had been mostly hollow. Yet it had seemed so healthy and strong with its thick leaf cover, not even hinting that it was slowly dying and near the terminus of a long and productive life; it had seemed to be the foundation of stability and endurance.

The inside of the trunk showed signs of fire, how old I did not know. Although the thick bark of white oaks makes them somewhat resistant to small fires, perhaps there had been one or more fires of a higher intensity, enough to damage the sensitive living part of the tree just below the bark. This would have provided an entry point for insects and fungi, eventually rotting away the wood inside. After this happens to a tree, it is just a matter of time before a strong wind blows part or all of it down. Its branches were completely lacking of leaves and small twigs, indicating it had been dead for more than the previous growing season. If it had stood during the most recent summer, small twigs, if not leaves, would have still been present.

I felt fortunate to have shared with this tree a small portion of its long life. Another large white oak that stands at the nearby Little Red Schoolhouse Nature Center was estimated to be over 300 years old. If my tree were of a similar age, it may have been standing as a small seedling when Marquette and Jolliet passed in their canoes just a few miles north on the Des Plaines River in 1673, bound for the Chicago Portage and the Great Lakes—well before the first land would be cleared by European-American settlers for agriculture in Illinois. By chance, the tree managed to persist through the present automobile age and the resulting spread of nearby urban areas that continue to expand unchecked, remaking a landscape that has not changed so significantly since being shaped by glaciers thousands of years ago. Interstate 55, six lanes of continuous, roaring traffic, and Mannheim Road, a main traffic artery through the forest preserves to the sprawl of the southwestern suburbs, lie only a short distance away. Yet this tree was not cut to make room for more development. Undoubtedly, preservation of the area as a forest preserve for the last several decades has had much to do with this.

But the old oak left many progeny. Most of the smaller white oaks nearby are probably its descendants. So, in a way, it lives on. As I return to this area over the years, the grand old oak will slowly decay to the earth, to become part of the soil; its stored nutrients will be taken up by other plants, which will themselves eventually return to the soil. Perhaps one day, decades from now, I will return, and there will be little sign of the tree at all. I will have to find new landmarks to help guide my trail. But hopefully I may with fondness recall the halcyon days of my younger years, and remember the great horned owl, the sandhill cranes, and the osprey. Maybe I will see their descendants as well.

Eulogy for an Oak

Backwaters, wetlands, and bur oaks

Side Channels

24

Drawn to Antiquity

In Cass County, Illinois, just east of Chandlerville, I stood upon the promontory of a steep, south-facing hillside covered with prairie grasses, wildflowers, and shrubs. It was a tough climb to this spot, fighting the thorny brambles and thick vegetation, but it was worth it to see the expansive view of the small creek valley, where hawks would sometimes glide past at eye level. All that I saw, except for the small hill prairie where I stood, was forested. But I knew that there were other hill prairies in the area, and that all of them were mere remnants of much greater grasslands that once covered the flat uplands and rolling hills of central Illinois. I am drawn to this hillside and others like it for the view and the wildlife, but also for its connection to a far distant past—before Illinois, before the Europeans—to antiquity.

Twenty thousand years ago, when there were glaciers, arctic tundra, and boreal forests, there were no prairies in Illinois. After the glaciers retreated northward, and when the climate became much warmer—warmer than even the present day—the prairies, encouraged by wild fires, expanded into Illinois from the west. Of course, agriculture and modern civilization have long replaced the grand prairies of central Illinois, the once rolling grasslands that extended to the horizon. So the remaining hill prairies—too steep to plow and difficult to build upon, original prairies planted by no one, that remain much as they have been—are true relicts of an ancient landscape that has been mostly lost.

As I have gotten older, I have become increasingly drawn to that which exhibits age. In architecture, music, books, landscapes, and even people. How different from my views as a youth, when new always seemed best; when it seemed that even our new music, generated on an almost assembly-line regularity, was superior to anything that came before; when the open, superficially clean, widely spread suburban areas could easily be preferred to the closed-in, noisy, antiquated central city of Chicago and its older suburbs. While focused on new innovations, as a young man looking toward his future and wondering about the possibilities, reveling in the "Space Age," I failed to fully appreciate the fine qualities of age, how a connection to the past could add a special flavor and context to my surroundings and experiences.

At middle age, I have reached the point where, should I live a normal life span, the years behind likely outnumber the years ahead. So I have begun to see the past not as something to draw away from, but as an invaluable archive of scenes and experiences from which to draw a deeper understanding. Newness by definition cannot have survived the myriad tests of time necessary to draw out hard-won qualities of integrity, strength, and durability. And valuing these qualities, I more often than not find myself seeking that which has survived a long and varied history.

These days I am quite aware that when I stand upon a high bluff top overlooking a system of ravines, hills, and river valleys, a hill prairie at my feet, I stand upon the cumulative result of the ages, upon a vegetation formation that existed long before I was born, long before my ancestors or the ancestors of most everyone I know traveled to this continent from elsewhere; a formation that I hope will remain for all future generations, even aware as I am of the inevitability, and perhaps desirability, of change. The power in the air at such moments is more than barely perceptible.

Side Channels

Hopewell Hill Prairies Nature Preserve, Illinois

25

A Western Birding Excursion:
Of Wind, Rain, Rocks, and Renewal

Usually after several years of not traveling much out of the Midwest, I develop a longing to see something different: birds and ecosystems, as well as cultures. For years the Colorado Plateau (centered on the Four Corners area of Utah, Arizona, Colorado, and New Mexico) has repeatedly drawn my attention; yet I had not been back for over a decade. So on a snowy, cold January evening in 2001, I made an early commitment to attend a volunteer service outing in April at Arches National Park, Utah. Then I spent the next three months planning my route and possible itinerary, all subject to change until the last minute.

Thinking of the West reminded me of all the bird species that I had missed on previous trips. I tend to miss species that others seem to find rather easily, probably due to my lack of focus or ambition to seriously look for specific birds, as a real birder would. One species, though, has gnawed at my conscience for over ten years: the ferruginous hawk. I may have seen one in Arizona in 1988; or maybe not; it was not a good, clear sighting. I traveled to the West again later in 1988, then in 1990, and again in 1997. No ferruginous hawk. I have long recognized that I may not be the most observant person, but missing a ferruginous hawk after so many visits to the West was beginning to get embarrassing. Though I may always feel inferior to the hardcore birding intelligentsia, I maintain that to lead a balanced life, it is probably best for me to avoid becoming too obsessed with finding new birds. Easier said than done? Perhaps.

* * *

After carefully packing everything I could think of (leaving behind the unabridged dictionary), I set out from central Illinois following a route designed to avoid traffic and large cities. In less than two hours I was west of the Mississippi River. But everything still looked like Illinois. At Swan Lake National Wildlife Refuge (NWR), Missouri, with its turbid water and levees, I could not help but feel that I was at Chautauqua Refuge in Illinois. It was not until I visited Prairie State Park in southwestern Missouri that I felt at least on the fringe of the West. One of the first birds I heard was a western meadowlark. Then, while sitting on a rock and contemplating a buffalo wallow (the park has a herd of free-roaming buffalo), for some reason, I turned my head and looked up at just the right moment to see a low-flying Swainson's hawk, a true raptor of the Great Plains. My trip to the West had a propitious beginning. I tried not to think about the ferruginous hawk except for the fact that I was probably still too far east to see one.

Because most travelers religiously follow the interstates, the county roads and two-lane highways tend to be lightly traveled, even on a holiday weekend. I stayed off the four-lane highways. St. Louis, Tulsa, Kansas City, and other big metropolitan areas remained merely names on a map. Avoiding their vast suburban areas and satellite subdivisions was difficult, though—noticeably more so than a decade earlier. Traveling the back roads also allowed me to maintain a certain intimacy with the land; it was easy to pull over at will if something caught my eye. As in Kansas, when I made a screeching three-point turn after seeing a scissor-tailed flycatcher sitting on a barbed-wire fence.

Beginning in Oklahoma, I pulled off the road for nearly every raptor that even remotely looked like a ferruginous hawk. Most were red-tailed or Swainson's hawks. In the old dust bowl lands of western Oklahoma, a kettle of several raptors soared over the highway. I quickly stopped. A farmer plowed his dusty field just below the soaring hawks, with the high winds picking up the dusty ol' dust and blowing it all away in a giant cloud. I stopped my tape of Woody Guthrie songs, shut off the engine, and proceeded to study each hawk; to my astonishment, they were all Swainson's hawks. One suddenly began to dive at another, and as both headed downward to the ground, I saw 40 or 50 more standing around a large carcass, very near the tractor's path. Only one bird mantled the dead animal and fed. The others hungrily looked on. Many were looking directly at me. The farmer, enveloped in the swirling dust, seemed to ignore both the hawks and me. Through my spotting scope, I carefully looked at each hawk, thinking that surely one must be a ferruginous hawk, but all were Swainson's hawks! Soon the farmer must have gotten too near, because most of the hawks simultaneously took to the air, formed a giant tornadic kettle, and drifted northward on the wind and dust. The farmer kept plowing, and what could I do except continue onward? He didn't even wave.

The Great Plains is still wide, open land with few trees, especially the western plains. But it is not wild land. Public land is scarce, and cattle ranching is king. Most of the land is private and fenced for cattle. I don't like to trespass; so onward I drove, the open country begging to be hiked across, a ferruginous hawk probably over a nearby hill. But I continued to drive, until Oklahoma's 32,030-acre Salt Plains NWR.

Most of the Salt Plains Refuge is frustratingly inaccessible to the public. So although long hikes were out of the question, a few access points allowed for quiet wildlife viewing; quiet, that is, except for the maliciously blowing wind. At the official refuge shorebird observation platform I guess I should not have been surprised to find...well...shorebirds. There was a snowy plover among numerous peeps and sanderlings. And while closely watching a foraging common tern, almost too close for me to use binoculars, I noticed a distant osprey fly through my field of vision. Among the highlights at another part of the refuge were snowy egrets, a little blue heron, northern shovelers, green- and blue-winged teal, and a large foraging flock of American avocets. Salt Plains Refuge does not resemble Illinois, but the singing Carolina wren made me still feel too much of a connection with Illinois. I needed to go further. A proper visit to Salt Plains Refuge would have to wait until another year, perhaps during the sandhill crane migration.

Because of all the open space in the West, I naively expected the campgrounds to be spacious, spread-out affairs with campsites widely separated. But to my consternation, at most public campgrounds, space was miserly used at best. The state park campground near Salt Plains Refuge was too developed for my tastes, and the campsites were too close together with little screening vegetation. So onward I drove.

Later, from my motel room window, far removed from the hum of campground generators, I observed dark, nasty weather slowly moving eastward. Strong, dangerous storms blew across Oklahoma and Missouri, and into Illinois. I thought of my house under the shade of a large Siberian elm tree. Would it be there smashed under the tree upon my return in two and a half weeks? But that was eastward thinking. I was full of hope and heading west.

Black Mesa Nature Preserve is at the far northwestern corner of Oklahoma's Panhandle. In terms of wildlife and plants, Black Mesa is an extension of the Rocky Mountains. Shortgrass prairie with pinyon pine, sagebrush, and Rocky Mountain juniper finally took away all thoughts of

A Western Birding Excursion: Of Wind, Rain, Rocks, and Renewal

Illinois. And Black Mesa is in the Rocky Mountain time zone. I hiked to the top of the mesa, all the while listening to western meadowlarks, and had to track down an unknown song to find a brown towhee, a species I had never seen before. Overhead, ravens soared and croaked on the strong and continuous winds. There were turkey vultures and red-tailed hawks. A large flock of pinyon jays flew across my path several hundred yards ahead. But I noticed, as I had before in other arid regions, that birds were few and far between. I sat within a jumble of boulders, scanning the skies for raptors. A male northern harrier glided past. More ravens. Eventually, thoroughly bludgeoned by the chilly wind, I shouldered my backpack and began the descending climb, at least a two-hour hike to the parking area.

By New Mexico, I almost gave up trying to find a suitable campground. Perhaps the park designers all studied their trade in the shopping malls of Illinois. Maybe they think campers actually want to see and hear everything that other campers are doing, and which television show each is watching. That is not where my interests lie. So with unenthusiastic resignation I planned to spend yet another night in a motel, but now I wanted a motel near a Mexican restaurant. Toward that end I plotted a course for Santa Fe, with a brief stop at Las Vegas NWR, New Mexico.

Public access at Las Vegas Refuge is severely limited. But the refuge has several artificial ponds that attract migratory waterfowl, plus an auto tour from which the ponds may be viewed. It was far from a wilderness experience, but, especially in the West, water equals birds. At an observation deck, not far from the parking lot, I observed numerous waterfowl of several species plus several eared and pied-billed grebes. Off in the distant grasslands, closed to public access, a group of pronghorn antelope lounged in the late afternoon sun.

Then, further along on the auto tour route, I stopped at a large pond, which was also very popular for bank fishing. I did not really expect to find much in the pond, considering all of the human activity. Yet not far from the bank were several western grebes, ruddy ducks, and canvasback ducks. I was slowly coasting along the dirt road looking for birds, driving with my knees and mostly avoiding potholes, when a cinnamon teal, a species I had never seen before, came into view not more than 20 feet away. I wanted to quickly stop, but another vehicle was behind me! After finally finding a place to pull off the road and backtracking on foot, the bird, of course, was gone. At that moment I knew if I finally did see a ferruginous hawk, the sighting would undoubtedly occur under the worst of possible circumstances, probably while driving on a busy, fast-moving, four-lane highway, a few seconds before the road enters a long mountain tunnel.

Later, on the interstate highway en route to Santa Fe, I had no choice but to forget about birds. Billboards and passing by slow drivers (anyone traveling under 75 mph) now occupied my thoughts. And gift shops, gas, and junk food. Santa Fe promised many motels and restaurants. But Santa Fe was not user friendly. Immediately upon exiting the interstate, I was swept up in a great cascading stream of traffic in the new suburban developments, with bright lights and confusing signs directing me everywhere at once; I was a rat in a maze. There was no time to think. The thought struck that maybe I needed new glasses. Why did I feel like a daft tourist in a foreign country? Was this culture shock, after exclusively traveling the back roads through small towns designed for people, not for automobiles? My original plan to avoid big cities was a good one. At Santa Fe, I strayed from the right path, and in only a few more days the service outing would begin, when looking for birds would become a lower priority. It was time to get serious. But first, Mexican food was the highest priority.

Santa Fe was quick and painless. Traveling quickly, I soon found myself on the Navajo Reservation in Chinle, Arizona, near Canyon de Chelly National Monument. To avoid the other curious tourists, of whom there were many, I checked out of the motel before sunrise. After driving several miles to a designated observation point, I walked a short trail that led to a

A Western Birding Excursion: Of Wind, Rain, Rocks, and Renewal

canyon overlook, where Anasazi ruins were visible several hundred feet below. Later in the day, paying tourists would be shuttled in large groups to the distant ruins of the "Ancient Ones," ancestors of the modern day Pueblo tribes, on open trailers driven by Navajo guides, like a well-oiled theme park. I sat in the early morning light, on the edge of a sandstone cliff, watching white-throated swifts, violet-green swallows, ravens, and a highly energetic spotted towhee singing one song after another. Then long before the turkey vultures rode the canyon winds, I was bound for another Anasazi site at Hovenweep National Monument, Utah.

The campground at Hovenweep was nearly deserted. I quickly set up my tent, and was on the trail, embarking on a hot, dry hike to a remote Anasazi outpost. I had plenty of water, a bird guide, and a copy of *Lonesome Dove*, by Larry McMurtry. Although soaring raptors would be difficult to spot in the cloudless skies, with an isolated campsite to return to, I remained optimistic.

As expected, in the middle of the afternoon, birds were as scarce as ever, but rock wrens sometimes sang from the tops of the desert bluffs. And from the gnarly vegetation, a black-throated sparrow or plain titmouse occasionally sounded off. A mountain bluebird was an unexpected sight, helping to maintain the afternoon's spirit of optimism. But except for the dependable ravens, the skies seemed empty. I panned and panned, thinking that a ferruginous hawk must be soaring above. But after returning to camp six hours later– still high from the great pleasure and privilege of being able to scrutinize a large, remote group of Anasazi ruins with no other visitors—the ferruginous hawk remained elusive. Like being tossed a bone from the desert spirits, a common poorwill sang a few notes just after sundown, just before the wind began to blow, a terrible wind that would blow birding and optimism to an oblivion for the next two days.

Though it may have been an illusion that wind increased as I traveled further west, it was no illusion that the land became rockier. Rock formations of startling proportions occupied views in all directions, in a landscape of stone and dusty, rocky soil. Overused phrases such as the "bones of the earth" can be pardoned as being simply the best description. It is in this area that the late Edward Abbey began his "...lifelong love affair with a pile of rock." The Colorado Plateau is, at least on the surface, one big pile of rock, but it immediately challenges the mind to comprehend its great range of scales. At one moment, the place seems vast in both time and space, endless and empty; while at the same time we are warned about our next moves, to stay on the official trails and avoid stepping on the sensitive cryptobiotic soil, an unusual association of bacteria, algae, lichens, mosses, and fungi. Damaged cryptobiotic soil could take years to recover from a footstep.

At Canyonlands National Park, Utah, the winds continued to blow, probably gusting to 50 miles per hour or more. In an entire afternoon of hiking, the only birds I saw were a few ravens and turkey vultures. The wind swallowed up all sound. So the immediate task was to find water, where there would also be birds.

The Scott M. Matheson Nature Preserve in Moab, Utah protects 875 acres of rare wetlands along the Colorado River. Tamarisk, a non-native tree that is literally taking over western riparian areas, is also found in the preserve. Tamarisk forms dense, monocultural stands in which branches from neighboring trees interlock to form impenetrable thickets. Most of the preserve is free of tamarisk, but along the Colorado River, there is little else. I hiked along the river on a maintained trail and was surprised to see two mallards take flight from the turbid water and a school of non-native common carp sucking air from the water's surface. The Colorado River began to seem more like a degraded river, and I became a bit depressed. Were it not for the many birds seen at this site, including a Bewick's wren and Townsend's solitaire, my disposition for the day would have been even more mixed.

* * *

True to my expectations of the service outing at Arches National Park, I did not find much time to pursue birds. We repaired trails and broke rock with pick axes, and told park visitors we were being punished for walking across the cryptobiotic soil; we hauled out tamarisk and transplanted bunch grasses and prickly pear cactus to help restore an area where an underground water pipeline had been installed. It was hard work, dry and hot work. On one day, I drank over a gallon of water. It was great!

Midway through the service trip, our leader granted us a free day, which I used to follow a watercourse that led to a seldom visited, remote part of the park. All day I looked up at towering sandstone cliffs with strange eroded formations called hoodoos. Birds in the riparian woods were sparse by Illinois standards, but by then, I knew what to expect, and so was not disappointed. Spotted towhees sang throughout the day, and blue-gray gnatcatchers, ruby-crowned kinglets, and yellow-rumped warblers (Audubon's variety with a yellow throat) were never far away. Near the furthest extent of the hike, while sitting against the stream bank reading, I looked up at just the right moment to see a distant flock of Brewer's blackbirds as they flew quickly over the wash and over the canyon wall.

On the return hike, I walked at a slow pace, knowing it might be many years before another visit to Utah. Life gives us only one chance to see the world, and I had yet to travel beyond the contiguous 48 states and Ontario, Canada. If I had not been looking downward as much as up—so as not to trip, step in water, or walk off the trail—I might have missed the shadow caused by a golden eagle move across my path. But the eagle was quickly beyond the canyon wall and out of sight. And such is the case with my birding style, and why I tend to miss species. Sometimes, however, the birds find me.

So if I were only prepared once in a while, life would be much simpler. On one of the final workdays, I had to rapidly walk a couple hundred feet to retrieve my binoculars to confirm that the bird I heard was, in fact, a lark sparrow. That experience should have taught me a lesson that would have soon been put to good use, if I had known what was coming. But no lesson did I learn. Later, I was trying to gather a shovel full of "soil" to transplant some Indian rice grass, concentrating on placing enough weight on the shovel to break through the cement-like ground without falling over, when I noticed a few others in our group looking toward the sky. They were watching a large gliding raptor. Oh no! My binoculars were several hundred feet away! I dropped the shovel and ran for my backpack. But by the time I located the bird, it was much further away, though still close enough for some plumage details...which showed that this bird was definitely not a red-tailed hawk. Of course, it was the ferruginous hawk. Then, all too quickly, the bird was gone, gliding over the canyon walls. Yes, fortunately, sometimes the birds find me.

After the service outing ended, I would have only the next two days to drive from Utah to Illinois before it was time to return to work (i.e., gainful employment). The return trip was, to say the least, swift. I remember seeing a black-billed magpie somewhere in the Rocky Mountains; Kansas was windy; and I heard the first eastern meadowlark of my return trip in western Missouri.

Before too long, I was soon on the edge of a rock outcropping at Trail of Tears State Park, Missouri, looking down on the Mississippi River and across at Illinois' Shawnee Hills, putting off the inevitable just a little longer. I listened to parula, yellow-throated, and Kentucky warblers, wood thrush, scarlet and summer tanagers, and more. On the river, a fish crow called as it stood on a log, floating downstream; a Mississippi kite glided over the river, and soon passed out of sight behind the river bluffs. It was not bad being back in the Midwest.

With almost 4,500 miles behind me and several new bird species, especially the ferruginous hawk, I felt satisfied. The West had grudgingly yielded a few more of its secrets. Untold secrets will continue to draw my attention. For I know that I will not be able to stay away from the Colorado Plateau for too long. So am I now in love with a pile of rock? Why not? A pile of rock offers no disappointments and cannot break a heart. For a time, though, my interest in the Midwest has been renewed. Without doubt, the Midwest also has many secrets yet to be revealed. Onward then—to Illinois.

Side Channels

Middle Mississippi River at Trail of Tears State Park, Missouri

26

Ties

The birds are the others, appearing so alien from us in every way. Most people might not ever try to understand the lives of birds, assuming that we can never know exactly what their thoughts are, or even if they have any. So different from us the birds seem. Yet as I peer into their lives in the quiet and still conifer forests of the Cascade Mountains, I perceive a kinship, one which shows me that our basic motivations, fears, and emotions are very similar.

It is after the hectic breeding season, when all young have left the nest, yet responsibilities for some parents continue. Certain young birds are still being fed by their parents, extending their adolescence for as long as possible, though they are physically capable of fending for themselves. A dark-eyed junco along the trail is feeding an insect to its young. The young bird then continues to quiver its wings, following the adult through the treetops. This seems on the verge of harassment; it looks as if the parent is annoyed, at least I would have been. *Get a job*, I'd say.

* * *

I walk for long periods now seeing few birds; many keep a lower profile following the breeding season and are difficult to find. Others gather into family groups and mixed-species flocks that travel through the woods together seeking food on bark, leaves, and the forest floor.

Suddenly, as I enter a red alder thicket, I am surrounded by a group of chattering chestnut-backed chickadees. The friendly chickadees keep a wary eye on me while going about their activities, and constantly call back and forth to one another. Their behaviors attract a winter wren and a golden-crowned kinglet; the wren seems to glare at me from within the thick foliage, as if demanding to know my business, and would I please move on.

I leave the alder thicket and enter an area of mature forest; the tall columns of hemlock and fir trees allow little light to reach the forest floor, and their foliage absorbs the wind and sound. Ahead is a family group of curious gray jays. They silently glide from tree to tree and to the dimly-lit forest floor, whistling encouragingly soft tones to each other as if to say that all is well, and ignore the big hairy beast. A Swainson's thrush appears unconvinced and continues giving an alarm call, even while holding a large insect in its beak. I hate to be such a disruption and feel a fleeting sense of unnecessary guilt.

* * *

Later, I come upon another group of jays, who at first behave similarly to the first group. But suddenly, a few of them high in the tree canopy emit discordantly harsh sounds of near-panic. The smooth serenity of the deep forest is shattered. Again I feel guilty, and wish I could tell the birds I mean them no harm.

But then I see a movement in the treetops: a hawk! A sharp-shinned hawk, predator of...birds! The jays knew it all along. They mob the hawk and create such a commotion that I start to side with the hawk, and almost cheer when it takes flight to make a quick grab at a brash young jay, intent on counting coup. The attack fails. The hawk flies off, and I get a flashing glimpse of the dispirited raptor. Perhaps the jay had learned a lesson. But the hawk may have also sharpened its skills. The jays should remain attentive, if they know what is good for them.

Further along the trail, I come upon a small mountain lake; tens of thousands of insects fly back and forth just above the water. There is an abundant trout population in the lake; the fish can be clearly seen, even at greater depths, and they continually leap out of the water after the insects. To all appearances, the lake is a healthy ecosystem. But there are no birds. Why are there not scores of swallows, warblers, and flycatchers, gorging themselves on the thick mass of flying invertebrates? Optimistic, I wonder if most species have simply left for southern wintering areas. And I realize that my understanding of nature is far from complete.

Someone once said that any animal knows more than we do. I don't know about that, but on this day I have been reminded of the ties between the natural world and myself. And as a result, I have become richer and more knowledgeable.

Side Channels

27

From a Great Lakes Journal:
Of Sand, Glaciers, and Birds

...the dunes have long afforded a refuge to human derelicts who have fled from the busy world of strife and turmoil to the peace and quiet of the sand hills.
–Milo M. Quaife, from Lake Michigan, The American Lakes Series, 1944

In central Illinois, I sat on the ground at my favorite hawk-watching perch, on a large sand dune overlooking the Illinois River valley. The sand, the geologists tell us, was brought down the river valley in a massive torrent of glacial melt waters some 15,000 years ago, and then blown into dunes by the prevailing winds. Many gulls soared over the river that day, but the skies were lacking in raptors. My thoughts drifted northward, toward the great sand dunes along Lake Michigan's shores, and so I began to make plans. Instead of waiting for the fall migration, I would wander around Lake Michigan, searching for birds, but in a loose, meandering sort of way.

Side Channels

* * *

While en route to Michigan, about ten miles to the east of the Mason County sand areas, I passed over a landscape that abruptly changes from a flat plain to gently rolling hills. This band of hills, thoroughly dominated by row-crop agriculture, forms a crescent across much of Illinois. It is the terminal moraine of the Wisconsin glacier, where the ice sheet, about 20,000 years ago, melted as quickly as it slowly moved across the land; the melting ice left behind a variety of materials, from dust to boulders. There were few birds over the farmlands, but I knew that in late September, they were surely on the move. Yet for the time being, I closely focused on arriving in southwestern Michigan before dark. Soaring turkey vultures and American kestrels perching on telephone wires were among the few species keeping the drive interesting.

In a flash, I crossed the Kankakee River, still in the Illinois River's watershed, in northern Indiana. For a time, I forgot about birds, caring only for the highway, nearly desperate to get away. But before too long, I became aware that the rivers I crossed flowed into Lake Michigan. The Illinois River's watershed, with its Gulf-bound streams, was behind me. So, like a rocket ship finally entering a stable orbit, I powered down and relaxed. A few ring-billed gulls lazily flew in the northwest. From their height, I supposed that they had a view of Lake Michigan, now only a few miles away.

Growing up in the Chicago area, Lake Michigan—what most simply call "the lake"— seemed to be at the center of my orientation in the world. The sun set in the western sky; the lake was in the east. Near the lake, it was cooler in the summer, warmer in the winter, and more snow accumulated—the famed "lake effect" snow. In lower Michigan, though, the lake is in the west, and this turns my world upside down; it is my personal Bermuda Triangle. I tend to head south when I would really like to go north; west when I mean to travel east. Even as I was acutely aware of this curious effect, the current trip provided no exception. To find Warren Woods Natural Area on a map, I pulled off the road, and then closely checked the road signs and the sun before proceeding cautiously.

Warren Woods is a true classic, old-growth forest. At about 300 acres, it is small even by Illinois' standards, but my imagination easily expanded it outward to the millions of forested acres that once covered a great part of eastern North America. The immense sugar maples, red oaks, and American beech, with the Galien River flowing beneath, inspired the final power down from my previous intense focus on covering the miles. With the sun nearing the horizon, I slowly walked toward my favorite tulip tree, about four feet in diameter, and probably the tallest tree for miles around. Red-headed woodpeckers called from several directions, already setting up winter stores of acorns and beech nuts.

I made only one wrong turn after leaving Warren Woods, and then headed back to the town of Sawyer. Beyond the motel room window, a crow perched on a utility pole, calling to a companion; a continuous stream of vehicles that would continue unbroken all night passed on the interstate highway; the sun had set over the tree line—and, I imagined, beneath Lake Michigan's continuous horizon of water.

At Warren Dunes State Park, I followed the back country trails to the lake, like a derelict keeping to the shadows, completely avoiding the main parking area with its crowds of beach enthusiasts. The trail led through an area of forested, stabilized sand dunes. Most of the forest birds were in mixed-species flocks, following the lead of the resident black-capped chickadees. Near the top of one forested dune, I sensed the wind blowing somewhat more vigorously, an indication that the lake was not far beyond.

As Lake Michigan came into view, the wide panorama of endless blue sky and water erased all thoughts of the modern world and its many intractable problems. I followed a deer trail to a lone cottonwood surrounded by a prairie of flowers and dune grasses, then sat under the tree for a couple of hours, attempting to gather in all the myriad sounds, smells, and colors. The continuously blowing wind gave rise to enormous swells far out on the lake, which eventually arrived at the beach, pounding its sandy shores, one powerfully breaking wave after the other. The pure white of herring and ring-billed gulls clearly contrasted against the white caps and deep blue waters as far as I could see. I scanned the skies for raptors riding updraft winds. Yet despite my conclusion that it was the perfect day for a raptor migration, only turkey vultures were numerous. A few red-tailed hawks soared like leisurely foraging residents rather than seriously moving migrants.

Before hiking to the water's edge, about 200 feet below my vantage point, I scanned the distant meeting of sky and water with my binoculars, and was stopped cold as I viewed the tall buildings of downtown Chicago, about 60 miles away, shimmering ghost-like in the vaporous air just above the roiling water. Since first viewing Lake Michigan earlier in the day, I had felt to be in the most peacefully secure location on the planet, where only the natural world mattered; now the sight of the tall skyscrapers allowed the rest of the world to intrude, and I wondered whether I would ever again be able to look at skyscrapers on a sunny day without thinking of news footage from that terrible September day in 2001.

The rest of my walk was complicated by a mix of emotions. Even the sanderlings, comically running up and down the beach at the edge of the dissipating breakers, failed to restore my former sense of equanimity. I needed true wilderness, and that was much further north.

For three days I camped at the 3,450-acre Nordhouse Dunes Wilderness Area located about 170 miles from the southern tip of the lake. Here I walked for hours along the sandy beach, encountering no one. Scanning over the water revealed not tall buildings, only more water and gulls. In my mind, our civilization became dwarfed by the powerful forces of the mile-high glacier that carved the Great Lakes out of the earth, the same glacier that dumped its load of debris as it melted in central Illinois, the same ice sheet that flowed in the other direction, a half a world away to Siberia. Compared to natural forces, our civilization, with all of its accomplishments and conflicting ideas, can certainly seem insignificant.

While in this thoughtful mood, a huge mute swan flew past. The mute swan is a European native, introduced to Michigan in 1919. And just after the mute swan, I noticed a few zebra mussel shells (a non-native mollusk accidentally introduced into the Great Lakes in the late 1980s) mixed in with the sand along the beach. I tried not to think about the fact that due to human influences the fish community of Lake Michigan has become a product of human re-invention and active manipulation. I tried not to think about the fish consumption advisories in effect for decades due to toxic contamination. This was a "wilderness," after all.

In the woods at Nordhouse Dunes, birds were scarce; but I noticed white-throated sparrows and dark-eyed juncos, which, given my location on the edge of their breeding ranges, could have been residents as well as migrants. To find more birds, I spent a couple of hours sitting beside the 30-acre Nordhouse Lake. The calm, clear, shallow water with its aquatic vegetation attracted a small group of waterfowl that contained mallards, black ducks, American widgeons, and Canada geese. In the space of a few seconds, a bald eagle, sharp-shinned hawk, and turkey vulture passed over. In vain, I waited for an osprey, only moving on after I thought of the great deal of ground yet to cover before dark. During the night, barred owls called and groups of coyotes howled and yipped. For a long time, I had forgotten about zebra mussels and mute swans.

The next day, as I drove northward, white cedars, paper birch, eastern hemlock, and white pines were becoming noticeably more abundant. At Hartwick Pines State Park, I briefly stopped for a short hike to view a small tract of woods missed by the loggers. Other than the glaciers, nothing has scoured the land in Michigan more thoroughly than logging. Though the paved walkway gave the old-growth woods a museum-exhibit-like quality, it was at this location, standing under a 100-foot canopy of hemlock, red and white pine, and sugar maple, that I heard the first raven of the trip. In the Midwest, ravens are associated with the north woods and wilderness. The mixed-species foraging flocks in these woods contained red-breasted as well as white-breasted nuthatches. On a continental scale, I had clearly crossed an invisible line into a different biological zone.

Continuing northward in rainy weather, I soon crossed over the Straits of Mackinaw to Michigan's Upper Peninsula (the "U.P."). Folks say that when one gives up trying that is when things begin to happen. So after giving up on finding interesting birds for a day, I guess I should not have been surprised to see a sandhill crane calmly walking across the interstate highway just north of St. Ignace. Fortunately, the traffic was sparse. So, leaving the crane to its fate, I steamed ahead for the famed Whitefish Point Bird Observatory, a bit concerned, though, about running into a tourist trap after seeing numerous "Visit the Shipwreck Museum" billboards along the roadsides.

Though the large parking lot at Whitefish Point was filled with vehicles and with people milling about the Shipwreck Museum, the bird observatory's visitor center was nearly empty. But my visit there was short, because as the weather cleared, I was highly anxious to be off on a remote trail somewhere. So while the museum looked interesting, and I hoped to visit it on another trip someday, I took only a quick glace at Lake Superior, and then wasted no time tearing out of the parking lot.

But the weather was soon again on the verge of rain. Though tempted to simply continue westward, no one who is interested in birds could visit the U.P. without a stop at Seney National Wildlife Refuge. Most of the refuge, including a 25,150-acre designated wilderness area, is either nearly inaccessible swamp or wetland, or closed to visitors. Before the rain began, I managed to hike over the short loop trail near the visitor's center and then drive around the 7-mile auto tour that follows part of the levee system. Here I was able to obtain nice views of trumpeter swans, which nest at the refuge, plus a variety of other water birds including pied-billed grebes, hooded mergansers, ring-necked ducks, and wood ducks. I saw no raptors, but with imminent bad weather, most were probably quietly roosting in trees, not searching for nonexistent thermals.

Continuous rain began soon after I left Seney Refuge, precluding all outdoor activities except driving. With occasional views of a mist-enshrouded Lake Superior, I followed Michigan Route 28 westward, arriving soon after sunset at the Silver Sands Motel, just outside Porcupine Mountains Wilderness State Park and across the road from Lake Superior.

In the morning, gray skies only inspired disappointment. It was the sort of day for inside reading. But I was determined to go on an extended hike, no matter what the weather might bring. In front of the motel, water pipits foraged along the roadside, and a bald eagle perched in a nearby tree. These were good signs, and at least it was not raining.

I followed Lost Creek Trail, one of the less popular routes into the park (most people enter at the famed Lake of the Clouds). The trail passes through an area of old-growth forest, totally missed by the loggers and miners. In fact, a large proportion of the 60,000-acre park was similarly missed. For the eastern states, an undisturbed forest of this size is a rarity; only Sylvania Wilderness Area, forty miles to the south, is comparable. I walked slowly and deliberately, listening for call notes. The forest interior would have been dark under any conditions, and with the heavily overcast conditions of the day, it was quintessentially dark, damp, and dismal. All day my wet shoes made a mushy, squashing sound on the well-worn muddy trail.

Birds tended to be grouped into loose foraging units moving throughout the forest. Within a short period, I saw golden-crowned kinglet, yellow-bellied sapsucker, white-throated and fox sparrows, brown creeper, and magnolia, yellow-rumped, and palm warblers. Then, for great lengths of time there were no birds. The call of a distant pileated woodpecker once broke the silence. I diligently looked for a black-backed woodpecker, in vain as it turned out, but not without at least one very tantalizing sighting.

It threatened rain all day, but rain never truly materialized. I fully expected to see at least one black bear, which also never materialized (they are fairly common in northern Michigan). In fact, if I had been more optimistic, I may even have expected to see or hear timber wolves, which are found in every county in the U.P. in no less than 60 separate packs.

But with more rain in the forecast, I once again left the wilderness behind for the highway, gambling for better weather by heading straight for Duluth, Minnesota, barely checking into a motel before darkness. In the morning, two horned grebes floated on the calm waters of Lake Superior as the bright sun raised the air temperature and burned away any remnants of lingering fog. Two sharp-shinned hawks flew directly over the motel. So I dawdled no longer and quickly followed the Skyline Parkway to the famous Hawk Ridge Preserve on a high cliff overlooking Lake Superior. The preserve allows easy access to several ideal lookout points, and these are typically crowded with hawkwatchers. But always the derelict, it seems, I found a less ideal location down the road away from the others. And with the skies filled with raptors, there was no need for an ideal lookout. Raptors were everywhere: broad-winged, red-tailed, sharp-shinned, Cooper's, harrier, bald eagles, and turkey vultures. Every few minutes, a low-flying sharp-shinned hawk passed overhead; and as I focused my binoculars on one hawk, I would see twenty more in the distance. Kettles of raptors formed one after the other. Occasionally, ravens joined with soaring raptors. There was also a large movement of blue jays, which passed along the ridge in groups just above the tree canopy. A tightly-knit flock of cedar waxwings once passed directly behind my lookout point, warily moving from tree to tree. Yet by early afternoon, anxious to camp that

From a Great Lakes Journal: Of Sand, Glaciers, and Birds

night at Sylvania Wilderness Area, I was headed back around the western tip of Lake Superior, downbound for the U.P.

At Sylvania Wilderness, I was home again, surrounded by a tract of virgin timber. Frost covered my vehicle's windshield in the morning, but I owned the campground. And although the first day remained heavily overcast, not quite threatening rain, common loons were constant companions that I either saw or heard as I canoed the length of Clark Lake. Croaking ravens, soaring bald eagles, and gray jays solidified my wilderness state of mind.

Yet after only two idyllic days at Sylvania, the weather, as a matter of course, quickly deteriorated. Without enthusiasm, then, I began the final leg of my journey back to Lake Michigan and then home. But first, I stopped at Horicon Marsh National Wildlife Refuge, about 40 miles northwest of Milwaukee, Wisconsin.

The night before, the calls of Canada geese were the last sounds I heard before entering the motel for the night, and their calls were the first sounds I heard outside in the morning. At the 21,000-acre Horicon Refuge, Canada geese numbered in the thousands, streaming inward toward the refuge from all directions; and their numbers were nowhere near peaking (over 200,000 at one time are not uncommon). Sandhill cranes and American white pelicans were also quite numerous.

I sat with the morning sun at my back on the glacial moraine hills that surround the marsh. And I recalled that the marsh was once a lake, which had its bed scoured out by a lobe of the Wisconsin glacier between 12,000 and 70,000 years ago. From this vantage point, with thousands of birds to watch, I chose to focus on the red-tailed hawks. In the steadily blowing winds, they gained sufficient lift by merely positioning themselves into the wind in such a way that lift exactly balanced their rate of fall. For indefinite periods, at least one hawk among many remained stationary hundreds of feet in the air. A slight wing adjustment caused a gentle drop or rise to a new desired altitude. These birds showed themselves to be true masters of the wind.

Although captivated by the hawks, for some reason, I felt anxious to get back to Lake Michigan, even knowing not to expect deserted beaches along Wisconsin's public-land-poor western shore. Along the boardwalk at Kohler Dunes Natural Area, Lake Michigan once again came into view. On the busy trail I felt crowded and strangely conspicuous in my filthy, scruffy clothes with ratty backpack and spotting scope. Wary folks on the trail nodded as we passed; but I, like any wild animal, avoided eye contact, and focused on marching straight for the beach. Then, just as I neared the water's edge, an osprey dropped from the air, making a big clumsy splash as it hit the water. The bird then flew low overhead, and was soon lost within a group of gulls. If I had not been there at that exact moment... sometimes, life is indeed good, even for a derelict.

* * *

Passing over the Des Plaines River on Interstate 294 near Chicago signaled that I was once again within the Illinois River's watershed, on the verge of being home. But before leaving Chicago behind, I took a quick glance at the downtown skyscrapers. I wanted to see them from the proper angle, with Lake Michigan on the east and the setting sun in the west. More importantly, I simply wanted to see them defiantly standing tall and strong.

The drive from Chicago to central Illinois and home was as uneventful as one can imagine. But in southwestern Tazewell County, just as the highway descended 100 feet as it left the terminal Wisconsin glacier behind, my thoughts again drifted northward to Lake Michigan and the U.P. The peace that I found among the birds and natural surroundings had not diminished as I recalled the previous two weeks. Peace by spending time with nature; it is an idea worth exploring.

28

Encounters with the Niagara River

One of my earliest recollections, probably as far back as the days when I could first comprehend language, is hearing about Buffalo, New York and Niagara Falls. Buffalo is ultimately where I am from. We moved to Chicago in 1960, and I have lived in Illinois ever since, but in 1957 I was born in Buffalo, at the eastern end of Lake Erie where it drains into the Niagara River.

Not until 1967, though, did I actually see Buffalo again, on a return trip with my brother and father, to see the old house on May Street in a quaint and safe neighborhood with shaded brick streets, and welcoming grandparents resting on the front porch. But beyond our visit with relatives, I also longed to see Niagara Falls, because I thought of the falls as one of America's wonders, in the same vein as the Grand Canyon, the Statue of Liberty, the Rocky Mountains; Niagara Falls was a place for entertainment, astonishment, and fear; a place of pure power on display. I recall now that I did not seem to think of the Niagara Falls as part of a river system that itself provides a connection between two of the Great Lakes—

Erie and Ontario—though my father may have educated me on these facts along the way. I was nine years old after all, and it would be many years before the term "drainage basin" was in my vocabulary.

This year, returning to Buffalo and the falls after nearly 40 years, I was not sure what to expect. I showed my wife, Julie, the old house on May Street, now with new owners and surrounded by a neighborhood that looked bombed out and finished, gang symbols on many of the buildings, broken or missing windows on most, a few others barely standing. But it was not this house or its trashed-up environs that drew us to Buffalo from central Illinois. It was the Falls, and a chance to see my aunt and uncle.

After our family visit, we approached the Falls not as one would travel to a single place to see an amusement park or a freak of the nation, but rather we traveled from the mouth of the 36-mile-long Niagara River at Lake Ontario, upstream to the Falls, in order to view them in context. At Lake Ontario, the Niagara River is about one mile wide and sluggish, giving no hint to the sublime ferocity, magnificent horror, and beauty only 13 miles upstream. From the walls of old Fort Niagara, we could barely see downtown Toronto, 30 miles across the lake; and in the other direction, the invitingly blue Niagara River gently curved to the right, with its variety of recreational craft lazily traveling to and fro.

From Fort Niagara southward to the city of Niagara Falls, we had few glimpses of the river. But soon we came to the top of a hill with the city in sight, and only the briefest view of a misty cloud hanging motionless in the river gorge: spray from the Falls themselves, where the entire Niagara River pours over a sheer cliff, reaching speeds of 68 miles per hour, falling as much as 173 feet.

For the first few miles below the Falls, the Niagara River is unnavigable, except for the famous "Maid of the Mist" tour boats that bring death-defying visitors into the spray of the Falls where the river is flowing fast and deep, as deep as the Falls are high. Downstream, the rapids of the

Niagara Gorge are as wild as any river could get; despite urbanization, tourism thrills and rip offs, and intensive use of the river for hydroelectric power, the river flows through the gorge as it will—white water, boulders, undertow, whirlpools, drawn by the force of gravity; water seeking its level.

Goat Island is located in the Niagara River, within the rapids and water racing to the edge of the Falls. Upstream of Goat Island, the river is rather placid, without much suggestion—except for the increasing rate of current—of what lies below. At the upstream end of Goat Island, there is a point called "The Parting of the Waters," where the Niagara River splits, 90 percent going toward Horseshoe Falls, the rest toward the American Falls. At the point of split, the current gives the impression of having stopped completely, appearing safe and inviting, especially on a warm day when a visitor would like to cool off. But one must not be deceived, for below the point terror is waiting, if one were to yield to temptation. The current rapidly speeds up to about 25 miles per hour, and quickly rolls over a series of rapids as wild as anything below the Falls. And in a short space of time, the edge is there, a point of no return, and a quick drop onto a boulder field designed by nature to leave no survivors—although over the years a few lucky souls have made the journey and lived to tell their tales.

The commercial exploitation of Niagara Falls for tourism is to be expected, and it is inescapable, with gambling casinos, bright lights, souvenir shops, and all the rest; but the natural forces driving the Falls are much greater and have not been overshadowed. As my wife and I stood in awe at the grand, rumbling spectacle before us, I recalled myself as a nine-year-old boy, gawking at the same view, and I thought about how that sight may have inspired me over the years, and how my perspectives on life, rivers, and the Falls have grown and become spirited with knowledge and enhanced with age.

Later, on the same trip, we stood on a footbridge over the Galien River, within an old-growth beech-maple forest at Warren Woods, Michigan. As I watched the slowly flowing waters beneath me heading toward Lake Michigan, I was suddenly reminded as never before of the connections; how those waters were destined to pass through Lake Michigan, the Straits of Mackinaw, lakes Huron, St. Clair, and Erie; past Buffalo in the Niagara River; past the "Parting of the Waters," to continue toward the point of no return, a minuscule part of the 4 million cubic feet per minute flowing over the edge so many miles away.

There are many places in this world worth visiting and many rivers I would like to see. But in my recollections and mind's eye, none are like the Niagara; it's where I came from, after all, and one day my wife and I shall return, though we may not wish to wait another 40 years.

29
Taking in the American Bottom

When thinking about the great diversity of river landscapes in North America, certain sites stand out from the rest because of factors such as an unusual historical importance or scenic beauty. Niagara Falls, the Grand Canyon's Colorado River gorge, and the Mississippi River's source at Lake Itasca come to mind at once. An area in southwestern Illinois called the "American Bottom" also comes to mind, but not for such obvious reasons. The American Bottom, in fact, is quite a curious area, a complex mixture or meeting of influences and consequences. This flat land of floodplain between distant bluffs is here because two of America's great rivers, the Mississippi and the Missouri, meet here. We also find in this spot clashing cultures, prosperity and poverty, prehistory and the present, waste and plenty, toxic and pristine, the violent and peaceful, all sending one's mind in myriad directions. But to understand the confusion, to take in the American Bottom as a whole, one must rise above the plain; and this is most effectively done at only one place, in my view, where everything can be focused and brought together in a manner that seems to make sense: at the top of Monk's Mound, a 100-foot-high earthen platform mound constructed by prehistoric Native Americans between A.D. 900 and 1250, at Cahokia Mounds State Historic Site.

So attempting to beat the rising heat and humidity of the day in late June, I awoke early and headed directly to Monk's Mound. Though I have visited this site many times before, as I approached the mound on this visit, its massive size once again took me by surprise; because for some reason, I always recall the mound smaller than its actual size of 14 acres at its base. This mismatch between reality and recollection adds to its mystique and to my sudden feelings of insignificance, something I have little doubt was in the minds of its designers. In fact, the power wielded by the elite rulers of the Mississippians who built the mound is still palpable. In stark contrast to the prehistoric images in my mind, there was a group of athletes on the steep stairway leading up the front of Monk's Mound; they were training for some upcoming event, I assumed, by running up and down the full stairway. They were quite focused on further tormenting their cardiovascular systems; yet even so, I could still not imagine any of them being completely unaffected by the location chosen for their sufferings.

Then finally at the top, the full expanse of the American Bottom came into view in every direction, from the Illinois bluffs on the east to the distant Missouri hills on the west. I felt as if I could reach out and touch St. Louis' Gateway Arch, though it was eight miles away. Interstate 55/70 roared on just below the mound, leading directly to the arch past the sadly poverty-and crime-stricken East St. Louis area. I discerned mere remnants of wetlands and streams in places, and knew that behind a particular line of trees was Horseshoe Lake, an ancient cut-off meander of the Mississippi River. Here at the American Bottom, over the centuries, the Mississippi and Missouri rivers have changed course here and there across the floodplain, leaving behind oxbow lakes, while flood-deposited alluvium has served to flatten the land. Horseshoe Lake is the most intact oxbow remaining. Old historic maps show the locations of many other lakes and wetlands in the American Bottom, most since lost to modern land reclamation to become rich floodplain farms, factories turned to rusted hulks of a bygone industrial era, home sites, roads, and acreage-gobbling warehouses.

I stood on the mound imagining the Mississippian society of some 20,000 souls brutally ruled by a minority class of totalitarian elites; those who have dug into some of the other mounds at Cahokia have found evidence of human sacrifice, mass graves, and mutilation. And some suspect that there was, indeed, quite a bit of conflict in what may have been a martial society. We may never know all of the facts; still, it is clear that the time of the Mississippians must have been dangerous. And although I stood upon Monk's Mound in safety and without fear, I recalled that our time also is dangerous, but on a grander scale and to a different degree. Would the next terrorist attack on U.S. soil, if one should occur, be deadlier than that which happened on September 11, 2001? Which despotic, tyrannical regime with weapons of mass destruction would be the first to attempt a launch? North Korea or Iran? China? Pakistan? Or someone else. Despite all of our modern knowledge and supposed sophistication over what came before, substantial parts of the world seem unable to escape the miseries of life under a seemingly inexhaustible supply of corrupt leaders, with the attendant poverty, violence, and strife. And I concluded that human nature has changed not at all across the years.

But those were not the thoughts that I wished to dwell upon at Monk's Mound. Then my attention was drawn to a little blue heron flying past at eye level, while an eastern meadowlark and blue grosbeak sang. The great chief of the Mississippians 800 years ago, at the very spot in which I stood, would have also seen little blue herons and heard exactly the same bird songs at exactly the same time of year, would have seen the same river bluffs, and felt the same heat from the sun.

And at that moment I became truly connected to the past and felt for a second that I was there, but then instantly determined that it was time to leave. Heat and humidity were building, and the athletes were climbing slower and looking more fatigued. A flock of turkey vultures rose on the first warm air thermals of the day, powered by the Mississippian sun, as I shifted my vehicle into gear. I harbored no naive illusions or nostalgic desires to have been born at an earlier time. For even with all of our worldwide problems, I have no doubt that our current era is still the best time that humanity has ever enjoyed. Confident and satisfied with my conclusions, then, I turned up the CD player and air conditioner, pressed down the accelerator, and drove off, without looking backward.

30

Isle Royale:
A Wilderness Island in Lake Superior

Cold winds blow across the harbor
Cold winds on the inland sea
Same winds that called our fathers
Cold winds calling me
–Tom Kastle, from the song *Cold Winds*©

Every spring, when the yellow-rumped warblers move through west-central Illinois and the songs of Swainson's thrushes echo throughout the oak-hickory forests, I think of Isle Royale in northern Lake Superior, the place where I first learned these birds' songs. My mind begins to fill with memories of previous adventures—as well as some misadventures—at the island that has helped shape my perspectives on life, such as they are.

Isle Royale National Park is an archipelago of some 200 islands, totaling 210 square miles, located about 15 miles from the Canadian mainland. The main island is 45 miles long and varies in width to a maximum of eight miles. It is an official federal Wilderness Area, and is internationally recognized as a Biosphere Reserve. This status gives Isle Royale a fair amount of protection from inappropriate developments. So except for the modest activities of the National Park Service, the hard-to-define quality of wildness remains intact.

Isle Royale's floral character is very different from Illinois, owing to its higher latitude, and this is also reflected in its bird communities, which of all things tend to hold my interest the most. Traveling north from Illinois, some of the first obvious traces of the north woods are natural stands of paper birch and quaking aspen trees that begin to appear at about Portage, Wisconsin; the abundance of these trees increases with latitude. By the time one reaches the Upper Peninsula of Michigan, the oak-hickory forests that are common in Illinois are left far behind. Here, the forests are dominated by sugar maple, white pine, and hemlock. Boreal forest conifers such as balsam fir and spruce are also abundant. One may expect to see a goshawk, as well as ospreys and bald eagles, during the breeding season. In summer, warblers that only pass through Illinois during migration will be singing on their breeding territories. A displaced Illinoisan has the feeling of being in a different world.

Traveling to Isle Royale requires a commitment in time unlike that needed to visit most of our other national parks, for it cannot be driven to or through. One must travel to the island by boat from Grand Portage, Minnesota; Houghton, Michigan; or Copper Harbor, Michigan; one can also fly to the island by seaplane out of Houghton. I usually take the Isle Royale Queen ferry out of Copper Harbor. Because the ferry leaves for Isle Royale at 8 a.m. (eastern time), it is necessary to arrive at Copper Harbor the previous day. My preference is to arrive in the early afternoon, allowing time to view the harbor area, where some interesting birds can always be found, and perhaps the nearby forested hills. Indeed, I once saw a merlin making a determined effort to catch swallows from a small flock that was foraging for insects above the harbor. The merlin, truly a bird of the northern forests, is a very agile falcon, but the merlin was no match for the swallows, which easily countered every one of the merlin's moves. Turkey vultures can usually be found soaring above the forested hills of the Keweenaw Peninsula in the same way their southern counterparts ride the air thermals above the cornfields of Illinois, but there the similarity ends.

Voyage to the Wilderness

Beyond Copper Harbor, Lake Superior was covered in thick, early morning fog, at times obscuring the division between air and water. The passengers were not festive as might be expected when on the verge of a summer vacation trip, but appeared rather somber. No one, it seemed, knew what to expect from the big lake, the largest body of freshwater (in area) in the world. As the boat left the protected harbor, the wind and waves picked up; the captain said it might be "a bit brisk" on deck, as the temperature of the lake, which never gets above the middle forties, keeps the air cool, regardless of the weather on the mainland. Superior, truly an inland sea, creates its own weather. The boat bounced around quite a bit, though not enough to make it uncomfortable. I spent most of the four and a half hours of the trip on deck, until I became chilled in the cool temperatures and wind. Herring gulls were interesting to watch, as they seemed to be following our boat across the lake, but inside the cabin there was free coffee with its needed warmth.

Just as the fog lifted, the big island came into sight, although it was still about a half-hour away. My plans were to stay at Rock Harbor Lodge for the first two days and then rent a canoe and camp in a remote area. After embarking, I sat on the back deck of my room for a while facing Lake Superior, re-gaining my strength and alertness that was lost to the winds of Superior. There were herring gulls and double-crested cormorants to watch in addition to the occasional common and red-breasted mergansers, common goldeneyes, and black ducks, some with young. It was strange to see the mergansers and goldeneyes during the summer months, as I normally associate these birds with winter (along with freezing toes and fingers).

Not less than 197 species of birds have been listed for Isle Royale. Of these, 120 are considered permanent and/or summer residents. Only 22 are listed as permanent and/or winter residents, an indication of the harsh winter conditions. The best way to see the most birds is to locate them by habitat type. There are eleven major bird habitats on the island, each with a characteristic bird assemblage, though most species may be found in more than one habitat. Other than Lake Superior and its shoreline, the spruce-fir-birch forest (boreal forest) is the most common habitat type on the eastern end of the island near the lodge. Without thinking about bird habitats, if one were staying at the lodge, most bird watching would then be done in the boreal forest, thus minimizing the search in other habitats. So I made a mental note to try to find as many other habitats as possible, so that I could locate species not characteristic of the boreal forest.

Although I was anxious to see as much as possible during my short stay on the island, I decided to take it easy on the first day by spending the afternoon on the Stoll Trail loop to Scoville Point, then taking in a Park Service lecture in the evening. The Stoll Trail is self-interpretive, with signs along the trail every so often explaining the ecology and geology of the island. It provides an excellent introduction to the island and also passes through several types of bird habitats.

The small forest dwellers, though, are difficult to view. As an example, all afternoon I had been listening to the incredibly complicated song of many winter wrens before actually seeing the bird. Because of the difficulties of finding a single singing bird, other species that are heard while trying to find a particular singer must essentially be ignored; I found myself having to ignore the black-throated green warbler in favor of the northern parula, only to be enticed by a loudly singing Tennessee warbler, a challenge to find under any circumstances. Trying to locate a Swainson's thrush was pure madness, but a good madness. Back at the lodge, there was a persistently calling least flycatcher cooperating very well by sitting on a treetop in full view, while several gray jays flew close by the front door of my room, where I had a fleeting glimpse of a pileated woodpecker. The yellow-rumped warblers were surprisingly easy to find; their songs will forever make me think of Isle Royale, the boreal forest, and Lake Superior.

My second day on the island, I awoke early for a quick breakfast. As I opened the front door of my room, I was greeted by the sight of a moose. During the next few days I would see many more. Isle Royale, in fact, has a large moose population, sometimes over 2,000, although the number varies from year to year. There apparently is no evidence that moose inhabited the island any earlier than the winter of 1912-13, when an ice bridge formed between the island and the Canadian mainland. Moose are strong swimmers, though, so some folks think they may simply have swum to the island.

Wolves arrived on the island about 1949, probably for the first time in history, by undoubtedly crossing an ice bridge. And for the last several decades, wolf predation seems to have kept the moose from too severely over-populating the island. Sick or old moose and young calves are the primary prey of the wolves. Though wolf numbers vary from year to year, and at one time they numbered 50 individuals, they may be slowly dying out. The most probable cause is inbreeding, which results in reduced reproductive success. If the wolves disappear, the moose will surely enter a cycle with population booms and busts, as they periodically overshoot the island's carrying capacity.

A Wilderness Camping Experience?

Side Channels

After spending two days as a pampered poodle at the lodge, I was anxious to camp on the other side of the island. To do this, I would have to cross Tobin Harbor and then portage a heavy 15-foot aluminum canoe and my backpack over the Greenstone Ridge 0.8 miles to Duncan Bay, described by some as the hardest portage on the island. It sounded fine to me, and I was on my way.

There was a thick fog over Tobin Harbor when I left. At times it was a white-out condition in the middle of the bay, and though I could not tell which direction I was paddling, I could at least tell, by the pull of gravity, up from down. A loon popped up out of the water about twenty or thirty feet away and gave its laughing call, a vocalization indicating stress. I thought, "Right, tell me about it." Finally, when I began the portage, it started to rain, then thunder and lightning. Birds were scarce in the rain.

Because of the heavy weight of the canoe, I had to stop and rest every few hundred feet of the 175-foot rise in elevation from Tobin Harbor. My heart was working overtime; I thought of the hundreds of pizzas I had consumed over decades and hoped that my heart and arteries were not completely encased in fat; yet all still seemed to be in working order and up to the task at hand. After setting up camp, I took the canoe out toward Blake Point along the Palisades, occasionally accompanied by several loons, about as far as I dared venture onto the open waters of Lake Superior, which seemed relatively calm for the moment. Singing white-throated sparrows were near the camp upon my return, and I looked forward to a night with only the sounds of the wilderness: wind blowing in the trees, owls and loons calling, perhaps even howling of the island's elusive wolves.

But that was not to be. A party of boaters soon arrived and set up their camp at the next wooden shelter. They were immediately loud, but to their credit on this one solitary point, one of them came to my shelter during the early evening festivities with an invitation to join them and share a few drinks. Though they were friendly, I politely declined, hoping they might be quieter as a result. But true to my expectations, their raucous yelling and laughter continued until the early morning hours, getting louder as they became drunker.

At first light, I awoke angry, vowing never again to camp at a site accessible to powerboats, and I quickly and noisily broke down my camp with plans to head for another site far away from power boaters. Then an osprey flew over as I left, improving my disposition tremendously.

It may be a sad result, but from this experience I learned to avoid disappointments on future trips by lowering my expectations, especially when seeking something so ill-defined as a "wilderness experience." So I decided to return to the Rock Harbor Campground near the lodge, via the dreaded Duncan Bay portage, in preparation for the next day's ferry trip back across the lake. On the trail, my spirits picked up when I saw cedar waxwings and a golden-crowned kinglet. And although it was difficult to observe birds while carrying the canoe, I did manage to hear an ovenbird and red-eyed vireo among many magnolia warblers. That afternoon a moose leisurely made its way around the Rock Harbor Campground, snacking on the lower branchlets of balsam fir saplings. The moose looked at me several times, yet seemed mostly unconcerned about my presence; I could not help being fascinated by the fact that this was a wild animal, prey for a pack of wolves, with no fear of humans. The moose apparently considered me to be a normal part of its surroundings, so perhaps at that point I was having a true "wilderness experience" after all. At any rate, it caused me to admit that such a concept is really just all in our minds, and can be defined however anyone may wish it to be.

Homeward Bound

I heard my last yellow-rumped warbler just before walking to the boat dock. When the Isle Royale Queen left Rock Harbor bound for the

Keweenaw Peninsula, I was sad, knowing it would likely be a long time before I would see a wild moose, or hear a gray jay, red-breasted nuthatch, or winter wren. I had yet to hear a wolf howl or see my first black-backed woodpecker. The island, though, would always be there; and because of the powerful legal protection, would remain much as I remembered it. It was a comforting thought. Luxury condominiums and noisy highways would never be a part of Isle Royale.

Herring gulls followed as our small craft left the protection of Rock Harbor for the open waters of Lake Superior. With Isle Royale in our wake, I could clearly see the lookout tower at Mt. Ojibway on the Greenstone Ridge, where on another trip I had hiked and had been almost trampled on the trail by a crazed moose and calf. And I know that that could have easily happened, because Isle Royale is not a fantasy theme park; it is the real world; just ask an old moose.

Far from the island, the large swells, one after the other, tossed our boat like a piece of flotsam, sending heads hanging over the side. And I recalled the foreboding aura in the air on that first day out of Copper Harbor. So it was like returning to the security of a warm fireplace after coming in from a blizzard when we finally entered the sanctuary of Copper Harbor, where the swells ultimately and mercifully stopped. As we passed the Harbor Haus German Restaurant, we were greeted by the synchronous kick-dancing of the waitresses arm in arm on the restaurant's outdoor deck, a daily tradition when the Queen returns safely. But that evening there was little doubt as to my choice for dinner: I would find a place that served pizza with extra cheese! Why change now? It has served me well over the years. And I must stay in shape for the next portage to Duncan Bay, when the migrating yellow-rumped warblers moving north through central Illinois, beckon me once again.

Epilogue

Thoughts on Twenty-five Years as a Naturalist

Alongside of my home, across the driveway, about an acre and a half of my own land is growing into a scattering of oak and hickory trees, red cedars, and hazelnut shrubs among dense prairie grasses, prairie wildflowers, and an odd assortment of plants left over from when the land was a working farmstead. We live in the Havana Lowlands, among the sand hills of central Illinois; and so I have begun referring to this land, though perhaps a bit prematurely, as Sand Hill Savanna. Its patriarch is a massive hickory tree, 3 feet in diameter and maybe 90 feet tall, which must surely have begun its life before the Lincoln era, given the slow growth of hickory trees in general and the even slower growth in our sandy soil. Multiple generations have made the decision to let this old hickory grow; I wonder how many in the future will do the same. The patriarch provides a tie to the far distant past, when sand savannas and prairies covered most of the land in this part of Illinois; while its progeny struggle with lack of nutrients and water, re-sprouting from occasional fires toward a future when my lifetime will be forgotten and left far behind.

Sometimes I will sit on our patio and gaze toward the old hickory and the slowly developing savanna, which improves in native plant diversity and community structure with every year, and I'll think about how all of this fits together and how many others might think about or even care about such topics. During these recent years, I do not feel as compelled to wander across the continent or escape among trackless wild areas as I did a quarter century ago. Of course, I am older today and recently married, both of which may have something to do with a modification of priorities. But I think my rather settled temperament of late has more to do with having discovered, over the years, a sort of harmony of mind resulting from a conscious effort to be closely tied to natural rhythms, wherever I happen to be, but especially at home. Home is the place I know the best: from the first red-winged blackbird song in February, to the peak of the Illinois River's spring flood, hordes of annoying buffalo gnats in early June, a changing panorama of flowering plants throughout the growing season, mudflats and shorebirds in August, kettles of migrating broad-winged hawks in September, multitudes of waterfowl crowding the river valley's floodplain lakes from late summer to the first freeze, and numerous other natural events; I feel a part of the whole. And this provides contentment, a calmness, and lack of estrangement from the natural world around me. In fact, the distinction between what is the "natural world" and what is not has, in my mind, become quite superfluous most of the time.

Some others who have made similar discoveries might soon become drawn to extreme activism, as they become focused on issues that are perceived as threats to the natural world as they define it—without the human component. I have stood at the entrance to this road, looked on with a critical, skeptical eye, but have not gone down; the politics and the egos, individuals and groups with agendas and their well-coordinated messages repeated at every turn, I find a disagreeable mix, a poor foundation for trust. So my interests continue to remain centered upon simply accumulating knowledge of how nature works, especially rivers and bird life; it is a task of personal satisfaction that can never be completed. It is what I started with long ago, and it has been enough to keep me going thus far.

Side Channels

Sand Hill Savanna at home

Acknowledgments

"Timeless Scenes along the Illinois River" appeared in *The Bluebird*, Volume 65, Number 4, 1998.

"The Eagle Quest" appeared in *Illinois Audubon*, Number 263, Winter 1997-98.

"Wings Over the River" appeared in *Illinois Audubon*, Number 269, Summer 1999.

"A Lesson in Nature's Dynamics" appeared in *Illinois Audubon*, Number 266, Fall 1998.

"Dead Trees, Disturbance, and Illinois' Red-headed Woodpeckers" appeared in *Illinois Audubon*, Number 274, Fall 2000, under the title "The Red-headed Woodpecker in Illinois."

"The Shorebirds Among Us" appeared in *Illinois Audubon*, Number 294, Fall 2005.

"When Hawks Fly" appeared in *Illinois Audubon*, Number 252, Spring 1995, under the title "Hawkwatching: A Glimpse into the Rhythms of Nature."

"Nature along the Margins at Cooper Park Wetlands" appeared in *Illinois Audubon*, Number 282, Fall 2002.

"The Gizzard Shad in Nature's Economy" appeared in *Illinois Audubon*, Number 253, Summer 1995; *Big River*, 1995, Volume 3, Number 12; and the anthology *Big River Reader*, published by *Big River*, 1996.

"Pursuing the Blue Goose Across Illinois" appeared in *Illinois Audubon*, Number 286, Fall 2003.

"Eulogy for an Oak" appeared in *Illinois Audubon*, Number 257, Summer 1996.

"A Western Birding Excursion: Of Wind, Ravens, Rocks, and Renewal" appeared in *Illinois Audubon*, Number 277, Summer 2001.

"From a Great Lakes Journal: Of Sand, Glaciers, and Birds" appeared in *Illinois Audubon*, Number 283, Winter 2002-03.

"Isle Royale: A Wilderness Island in Lake Superior" appeared in *Illinois Audubon*, Number 256, Spring 1996.